D0106086

Using
Behavioral Methods
in Pastoral Counseling

Howard W. Stone

NO LONGER PROPERTY OF
BRESCIA COLLEGE LIBRARY

Fortress Press   Philadelphia

BRESCIA COLLEGE LIBRARY
OWENSBORO, KENTUCKY

Creative Pastoral Care and Counseling Series
Editor: Howard J. Clinebell, Jr.
Associate Editor: Howard W. Stone

The Care and Counseling of Youth in the Church by Paul B. Irwin
*Growth Counseling for Marriage Enrichment: Pre-Marriage and
    the Early Years* by Howard J. Clinebell, Jr.
Crisis Counseling by Howard W. Stone
Pastoral Care and Counseling in Grief and Separation
    by Wayne E. Oates
Counseling for Liberation by Charlotte Holt Clinebell
Growth Counseling for Mid-Years Couples
    by Howard J. Clinebell, Jr.
Theology and Pastoral Care by John B. Cobb, Jr.
Pastor and Parish—A Systems Approach by E. Mansell Pattison
Pastoral Care with Handicapped Persons by Lowell G. Colston
The Care and Counseling of the Aging by William M. Clements
Anger and Assertiveness in Pastoral Care by David W. Augsburger
Using Behavioral Methods in Pastoral Counseling
    by Howard W. Stone

COPYRIGHT © 1980 BY FORTRESS PRESS

All rights reserved. No part of this publication may be reproduced,
stored in a retrieval system, or transmitted in any form or by any
means, electronic, mechanical, photocopying, recording, or otherwise,
without the prior permission of the copyright owner.

254.5
5877

Library of Congress Cataloging in Publication Data

Stone, Howard W
    Using behavioral methods in pastoral counseling.

    (Creative pastoral care and counseling series)
    Bibliography: p.
    1. Pastoral counseling.   2. Behavior therapy.
    I. Title.
    BV4012.2.S753   253.5   79-2287
    ISBN 0-8006-0563-2

7714H79   Printed in the United States of America   1-563

Contents

79731

Series Foreword

Let me share with you some of the hopes that are in the minds of those of us who helped to develop this series—hopes that relate directly to you as the reader. It is our desire and expectation that these books will be of help to you in developing better working tools as a minister-counselor. We hope that they will do this by encouraging your own creativity in developing more effective methods and programs for helping people live life more fully. It is our intention in this series to affirm the many things you have going for you as a minister in helping troubled persons —the many assets and resources from your religious heritage, your role as a leader of a congregation, and your unique relationship to individuals and families throughout the life cycle. We hope to help you reaffirm *the power of the pastoral* by the use of fresh models and methods in your ministry.

The aim of the series is not to be comprehensive with respect to topics but rather to bring innovative approaches to some major types of counseling. Although the books are practice-oriented, they also provide a solid foundation of theological and psychological insights. They are written primarily for ministers (and those preparing for the ministry) but we hope that they will also prove useful to other counselors who are interested in the crucial role of spiritual and value issues in all helping relationships. In addition we hope that the series will be useful in seminary courses, clergy support groups, continuing education workshops, and lay befriender training.

This is a period of rich new developments in counseling and psychotherapy. The time is ripe for a flowering of creative methods and insights in pastoral care and counseling. Our expectation is that this series will stimulate grass-roots creativity as innovative methods and programs come alive for you. Some of the major thrusts that will be discussed in this series include a new awareness of the unique contributions of the theologically trained counselor, the liberating power of the human potentials orientation, an appreciation of the pastoral care function of the ministering congregation, the importance of humanizing systems and institutions as well as close relationships, the importance of pastoral *care* (and not just counseling), the many opportunities for caring ministries throughout the life cycle, the deep changes in male-female relationships, and the new psychotherapies such as Gestalt therapy, Transactional Analysis, educative counseling, and crisis methods. Our hope is that this series will enhance your resources for your ministry to persons by opening doorways to understanding of these creative thrusts in pastoral care and counseling.

In this volume Howard Stone shares his extensive practical experience in using the theory and methods of the behavior therapies in pastoral counseling. For a variety of reasons, these therapies have received scant attention by those who teach and write in the field of pastoral care. The neglect of this rapidly expanding cluster of therapies has deprived our field of valuable resources for helping people grow by learning to cope with their problems constructively. This book makes some of the key concepts and methods of the behavior therapies readily available. It applies these resources to the kinds of problems and issues pastors confront in their work with troubled people. The book will serve as a practical introduction to behavioral methods both for pastors and for counselors from other disciplines who wish to understand and use these approaches.

As the author points out, behavioral approaches, to be used constructively, must be used within the context of a relationship of trust, empathy, and caring. The same principle applies, of course, to all approaches to counseling and therapy. Howard Stone emphasizes the fact that the goal of behavior-oriented therapies is not control over others but increased self-direction of one's own life. By relating behavior therapies to the theological heritage and to the community of faith within which ministers function as counselors, the author has made a crucial conceptual contribution which will encourage the creative use of these approaches within the church.

As counseling pastors, we are concerned with helping people learn constructive feelings, attitudes, and beliefs on the one hand, and constructive ways of acting on the other. For this reason the emphasis of this book on *cognitive*-behavioral therapies certainly increases the applicability of behavioral methods to helping people change both their growth-blocking beliefs and values and their self/other hurting behavior. I am struck by the fact that the first case-illustration in the book is an example of how a pastor helped a parishioner deal with the problem of meaninglessness (which hardly fits the usual stereotype of the limitations of behavioral approaches). The chapter on relaxation methods will be useful in many types of counseling situations. (It may also be helpful to us pastoral counselors in coping with our own stresses and anxieties.) The chapter on children should be valuable in helping parents help their children learn constructive self-discipline. It will also be illuminating to those who work with children and youth as teachers or counselors.

Until recently, Howard Stone had been director of an interfaith center for counseling and therapy in Scottsdale, Arizona. While in this post, he developed through actual practice impressive skills in using behavioral methods in growth-producing ways. He also provided leadership in developing an extensive program of training pastoral counselors including training in the use of behavioral methods. Shortly after completing the manuscript for this book, Howard accepted an appointment as Professor of Pastoral Care and Pastoral Psychology at Brite Divinity School, Texas Christian University, in Fort Worth, Texas. I am pleased that this significant new book happened to coincide with a new and promising chapter in his professional journey. Howard has contributed significantly to the literature in the field of pastoral care and counseling in his earlier writings, including *Crisis Counseling* in this series. In my judgment, this present book is his most innovative contribution to the conceptual enrichment of our field.

I have appreciated the opportunity to work with Howard Stone as we shared the editorial responsibilities involved in this series. Our collaborative relationship and the necessity to struggle together with the wide variety of issues and problems involved in this task has provided an opportunity to deepen our friendship.

As I have come to know him better, my appreciation of Howard's competence as a writer and as a practitioner of pastoral counseling has continued to grow. In this book he implicitly challenges some long-held and seldom questioned assumptions in the field of pastoral counseling as he offers some new options for the practice of this art. I invite you to open yourself to the thrust of the book and to its potential for expanding the horizons of your working conceptions and thus enriching your practice of effective pastoral counseling.

HOWARD J. CLINEBELL, JR.

Preface

If someone had asked me twelve years ago, while I was in graduate school, what I might write about in the future, I never would have suggested this book. I wouldn't even have dreamed of it. Although I had studied behavior therapy methods and was already practicing them in a limited way, it was the counselees I encountered over the last eight years at Interfaith Counseling Service in Scottsdale, Arizona who actually changed my counseling approach. In grappling with the challenge to do the most effective counseling possible for each of them, I found that I had to abandon some of my "favorite" counseling methods and begin to retool. This retooling focused especially on cognitive therapies and on further work in the traditional behavior therapies. The present book, then, is a sharing of some counseling methods that I have found beneficial for the troubled people I have encountered in recent years.

Most persons coming to a minister for counseling will not have bizarre and extreme mental disorders. Most are people whose difficulties simply involve distressing thoughts and behaviors, either their own or those of the people around them. Behavioral methods—whether used alone or in concert with the more traditional insight-feeling oriented approaches of pastoral counseling—have been found to be highly effective in alleviating such life problems and in freeing individuals to live as they would choose, to seek out joy and fulfillment in ways that have meaning to them, while growing in their faith.

Although these methods, like any others in counseling, can be abused when applied rigidly or in an uncaring way, they can be used well if they are followed as herein described and if they are accompanied by genuine empathy and concern for the client. Since this is a book on specific counseling methods, it does not address the important subject of the counseling relationship as such. Nonetheless, the quality of the pastor-parishioner inter-action is the foundation upon which the building blocks of all counseling approaches are laid. If there is not good therapeutic rapport, the best methods in the world will fail. The reader who is weak in establishing relationship with counselees is urged to do some work in this area prior to tackling the approaches explored in this book. Since the focus here is on helping an individual develop life skills necessary for resolving the immediate problem as well as future problems, these methods for the pastoral counselor are not to be applied in a mechanistic way, without feeling, but are to be used systematically and with great sensitivity in an environment of tenderness and empathy.

Behavior therapy, like any other counseling approach, is not beneficial in all situations. It simply makes available one more set of methods for the pastor's arsenal of counseling techniques. This little book, therefore, is not a comprehensive work on behavioral theory but only an introduction to selected behavioral methods. My hope is that it may spur the reader to further exploration of this vast and promising field of knowledge and practice. The goal is to help ministers become even more effective in giving pastoral care to their congregations.

While I am writing this preface Karen, my wife, is editing and typing chapter 5. Glancing up at her, I am reminded of several individuals who have helped in the book's preparation. I owe a debt of gratitude to the readers of the manuscript, Andy Garman, Gary Grassi, and Richard Lanyon. I continue to be impressed with my two colleagues in this series, Edward A. Cooperrider of Fortress Press and Howard J. Clinebell, editor of the series; they have done their tasks with excellence. I am also especially appreciative of Karen Stone, herself a busy artist and professor, who shared much of her vacation time with this book and helped to edit and prepare the manuscript. Thanks also go to Chris Stone, our daughter, for her cups of tea brewed, tasty meals served, and usually cheerful tolerance of my preoccupation with the project. And I feel much gratitude to Interfaith Counseling Service for allowing me the sabbatical time needed to work on the book, and to all those who have challenged me and thus forced me to clarify my thinking about behavioral methods. Finally, I want to thank Tom and Jeanette Alltop, at whose beautiful cabin on Lake Vermilion in northern Minnesota I wrote the first draft, and whose expert advice on "where they're biting" gave me something to look forward to each evening when the day's writing was done.

1. Behavioral Methods: An Introduction

Pastor Jacob had invited Raymond Carlson to come over for a talk. Both men were aware of the problem. Last Sunday Jim Carlson had come to the youth group at church intoxicated. The pastor wanted to talk with the father about the boy. Mr. Carlson, it turned out, wanted to talk only about himself.

"It's just one more thing," he mused, referring to his son's drinking and at the same time changing the course of the conversation. "Sometimes I don't even believe the things we talk about on Sunday anymore. It used to be so easy to believe. Now there isn't anything I really believe in. My wife is always busy with the kids or with the classes she's taking. She has no time for me! My kids are never around except when they want something from me. At work it's push, push, push—always deadlines. My boss is always on me. My staff doesn't seem to care about their work. Every day I have to clear up some mess they've made. I don't know. [Pause] I don't seem to get any joy out of living anymore. [Pause] You know, when you preached several weeks ago about how we all have to have some meaning in life? Well, I don't have it anymore, and ever since that sermon it's been gnawing at me. I've tried to get it back but I can't . . ."

Raymond Carlson was obviously troubled. Once he started talking, it was hard to stop him. He was indeed depressed, feeling trapped, left out of the family, caught in a vice at work; but what troubled him most was the loss of meaning in his life. He didn't feel nourished by life. He saw no challenge in his life. He no longer sensed God's wings of support or God's destiny for his life.

Raymond was in the midst of a deep spiritual crisis when he sat down to talk with his pastor. To one who was raised and nourished in the church all his life, repeatedly elected to leadership positions in the congregation, and involved in all sorts of parish

1

activities, this crisis was a shock to his whole system of values and beliefs. It was a shaking of his foundations.

Raymond's case is an interesting one from the standpoint of a book on behavioral methods in pastoral counseling because behavior therapy has often been considered inadequate in addressing existential questions. Yet Harold Jacob, who had received some training in behavior therapy methods, found that he was able to employ them as primary components in the short-term pastoral care he offered Raymond at this time.

Mr. Carlson actually visited with his pastor on only four occasions: when he first came to talk informally about his son, and on three subsequent visits formally scheduled during that first one. On the first visit, the pastor allowed Raymond to tell his story in his own way. So much tension was built up inside the man that he was not unlike a pressure cooker which, when it begins to whistle, takes some time to stop. After about twenty-five minutes of almost constant talking, Raymond finally let out a sigh of relief and exclaimed, "Boy, I guess I've had a lot on my mind; I think I'd better be going. I don't want to keep you anymore."

The inclination of a busy pastor at that point might have been to tell Raymond that it was good he could get these things off his mind, then to wish him well and get back to the mountain of work piled on the pastor's desk. Rather than take this "easy way out," Pastor Jacob responded: "Raymond, I'm concerned about what you have said. You seem to be carrying a lot of pressures on your back and seeing no way out of the problems. They could continue and possibly intensify. Maybe we need to discuss ways for you to resolve some of your struggles. If you will remember, one of the things I said in my sermon on meaning in life was . . ."

The two rehashed the sermon which had triggered such an emotional storm in Raymond. They discussed how it could be applied to his life. They then made a contract to meet with each other three more times (at this point the relationship changed from informal to formal, from pastoral care to pastoral counseling) and to do certain things: Pastor Jacob agreed to keep strictly confidential what was said in the sessions. He promised to serve as a consultant or guide to Raymond on his spiritual journey through his current crisis. Raymond in turn agreed to be honest about his situation, not avoiding hard-to-face facts, and to not just *talk* about his struggles but actually *do* something about them.

Many behavioral therapists put this mutual contract in writing, noting the goal to be reached, how many sessions they will have for working on it, and what both the therapist and client agree to contribute. In the case of Raymond and his pastor, the contract was verbal.

Once their counseling relationship was established, the goal of the counseling was determined: their common purpose would be to reestablish meaning in Raymond's life, inasmuch as Raymond felt that lack of meaning was at the core of his other problems. While this may on the face of it seem like a vague goal, perhaps too vague, in this case the two people involved understood it clearly, having shared a discussion of Pastor Jacob's sermon on the subject. The goal, of course, would continue to be refined throughout the counseling relationship. Frequently goals which begin as vague or unrealistic ideas gradually become more concrete, manageable, and realistic as the counseling progresses.

The next step was to work out an assessment of the problem to be resolved. Assessment is actually a part of most counseling methods, but in behavior therapy it differs in two significant ways: First, whereas in most traditional therapies the assessment (frequently called diagnosis) is solely the task of the therapist, behaviorally oriented counselors for the most part believe that the best assessment is done by both parties—client and counselor in collaboration. Second, whereas many traditional therapies focus on the "why" of a problem, what caused it to occur, the behavior therapist is looking for what *cues* (or stimuli) triggered the onset of the problem and what *reinforcers* (or rewards) are causing it to be maintained or continued. As one of my clients once said of her depression, "We're Sherlock-Holmesing this thing, aren't we?"

That was what Pastor Jacob asked Raymond to do: to observe himself and to write down precisely what these cues and reinforcers were, whether they were his own acts or those of his family or staff at the office, or just aspects of his surroundings not specifically related to any particular person. Such assessment requires complete, precise, and accurate recording. It was therefore suggested that Mr. Carlson involve his wife and even his Scrabble buddy in the process and have them too write down what they observed.

Finally, just before Raymond parted, Pastor Jacob predicted that some of Raymond's efforts at assessment would probably prove uncomfortable and that he "might want to avoid" certain troubling explorations. He urged Raymond instead to face them and to do as much investigation as possible, even in uncomfortable areas. Raymond left feeling relieved. He had gotten much off his chest in this first impromptu session, and with the program ahead of him he was beginning to feel that there was a "way out." He had a sense that he was going to be able to do something about his situation.

We will return at the end of the last chapter to Raymond Carlson to see how he and his pastor effectively utilized several behavioral methods which helped him carve out new meaning from a situation which had seemed so utterly hopeless a short time before. Raymond's situation is not atypical. How do we ministers deal with it?

Until twenty or thirty years ago the traditional pastoring methods of comfort, prayer, Bible reading, and admonition were our stock-in-trade. But the psychology explosion of the twentieth century created reverberations which were soon heard in the church. Sigmund Freud and Carl Rogers became required reading in seminaries. Client-centered therapy was the byword. Even the most flaming-radical, social-activist pastor, in counseling, practiced "mirroring"—reflecting back to parishioners the essence of their own feelings.

A plight like Raymond's was seen not as the agonies of one on a spiritual pilgrimage but as the struggles of one who had deep-seated psychological problems. The emphasis in the psychological age of ministry would have been to get beneath the surface situation, through nondirective or analytic methods, to release him from these "blocks."

Two problems arose as a result of this trend: First, the psychological and the theological were split; to be "psychological" meant not to refer or even covertly allude to the word of God.*

Second, although it is good that people in the ministry have learned from the field of psychology, they have listened only to selected voices in it, those assumed not to be hostile to religion, with the result that pastoral care and counseling lacks learnings from the most important movement in psychology since psycho-analysis, that of behavior therapy. But pastors dare not ignore these learnings simply because they may not on the surface seem congruent with Christianity or because they are not a part of our tradition in pastoral care and counseling.

The purpose of this book is to describe several of the basic methods of behavior therapy that are adaptable to pastoral care and counseling. Such practical methods for bringing change in behavior will be offered with actual cases illustrating how they can be applied, cases in which the names and identifying facts have of course been changed. Although the size of the book precludes a more extensive portrayal of the methods or an extensive delineation of the principles on which behavior therapy is based, the Annotated Bibliography at the end of the book does contain suggestions for further reading in these areas.

What Is Behavior Therapy?

One need not do more than open a newspaper or news maga-zine, turn on a late-night talk show, or walk into any bookstore to be confronted by the wide array of therapies vying for recog-nition. One can be Rolfed, sensitized, grouped, reality-ized, Gestalted, T-A'd, bioenergized, encountered, ested, or primal screamed—to name a few. Throughout church history a variety of psychological viewpoints have been incorporated into the practice of ministry. Today the array of therapies available to the minister is mind-boggling. Few of us have attended a min-isters' meeting without hearing a conversation in which someone has "found the answer" in such and such a therapy.

Behavior therapy is different from these popular therapies, as well as from traditional methods, in that philosophically it fol-lows an experimental approach to the understanding of human behavior. Human psychology is called the science of behavior because it assesses and tries to explain what individuals do and how and why they do it. Behavior is broadly understood to in-clude both the overt (observable) and the covert (not directly observable) elements of what human beings do. Behavior therapy develops practical therapy methods for helping individuals with problem of living, methods that are based on theories developed out of ongoing experimentation and research in the behavioral sciences. Behavior therapy thus is based on a solid and still-growing body of knowledge.

Although the roots of behaviorist psychology reach into the previous century, the use of experimental findings within the counseling session has only recently been explored. Marvin R. Goldfried and Gerald C. Davison rightly view the development of behavior therapy as a confluence of three diverse trends.*

The first of these trends is found in the work of pioneer behavioral psychologists O. R. Lindsey and B. F. Skinner, begun at the Metropolitan State Hospital in Massachusetts, which focused on controlling the hospital's environment (for example, by having patients attend meals on time and talking about "noncrazy" ideas) in order to change the behavior of its inhabitants. Hospital wards became gigantic "Skinner Boxes," a reference to the cages in which test animals (like pigeons and rats) were placed, cages equipped with controlling instrumentation to foster the training or conditioning of the prescribed behavior. In consequence of their pioneering efforts many of the grossly psychotic behaviors were successfully eliminated. Elsewhere Teodoro Ayllon was doing comparable research at the Anna State Hospital in Anna, Illinois.

The work of Lindsey, Skinner, and Ayllon was largely American. Arnold Lazarus and Joseph Wolpe in South Africa and H. J. Eysenck and M. B. Shapiro in London were also doing both experimental and clinical work, mainly with nonpsychotic individuals. Their work, which is regarded as the second of the three trends, focused on neurotic anxiety, its origins and treatment. Therapy emphasized what Wolpe called reciprocal inhibition. For example, they treated very anxious persons by training them to relax and then exposing them to graded doses of the very thing feared. This procedure, referred to as systematic desensitization, will be discussed more fully in chapter 5.

A final trend in behavior therapy corrects an early belief of some behaviorists that behavior is purely mechanistic, thus ignoring the covert behavior of the thinking or cognitive process.

Julian Rotter, Perry London, Albert Bandura, Albert Ellis, and others have reemphasized the importance of cognition in human behavior. This trend in behavior therapy, which will be discussed more fully in chapter 3, asserts that unadaptive emotions and behaviors are maintained by the unrealistic thoughts or expectations a person holds and that these thoughts can be changed.

Theology and Behavior Therapy

A principal difference between behavior therapy as done by a minister and behavior therapy as undertaken by a secular counselor resides in the minister's perspective. Although pastors may use the same methods as other mental health professionals, they approach the task from a different vantage point. Deeply troubled people almost invariably raise questions concerning death, pain, suffering, and meaning in life; all such questions are religious at their core and involve issues with which one must come to terms. Pastoral counseling is therefore in its final and basic concern spiritual. LeRoy Aden in *The Dialogue between Theology and Psychology* describes "final" as that which is ultimate in the end or climax of a process; "basic" he describes as being ultimate for an individual at a particular moment of time. He goes on to say that the final and basic concerns of the ministry differ from those of psychology in that "pastoral counseling has a different guiding image of . . . [our human] plight and rescue, and therefore it often perceives in the client's verbalizations a different struggle and end point."* Sharing with troubled individuals their hardships, failures, and despair can help one understand the meaning of such theological concepts as sin, grace, sacrifice, faith, and hope.

What is more, the minister's unique religious perspective as a counselor exists within a community of faith. This community includes and is more than a geographical area, more than a specific congregation of believers; it is an experience, a coming together of human beings through which each person's potential can be achieved. The community of faith must constantly be in tune with the word of God in each human situation. For example, bringing the word to a couple grieving over the loss of their child may mean no more than sitting with them, hearing their agony, and comforting them; it is not necessarily verbalized.

Wherever such a community exists, its minister is able to offer
to suffering persons the support and caring of *all* the members
of the household of faith.

Common Misunderstandings about Behavior Therapy

A major stumbling block to the acceptance of behavioral
methods within the religious community is the way they have
been perceived. Behavior therapy has been regarded as deterministic, mechanistic, simplistic, as brainwashing, shock therapy,
manipulation. Such labels readily suggest themselves when we
think of those vivid scenes from the movie *One Flew Over the
Cuckoo's Nest* in which all manner of atrocities were performed
upon the patients of a mental hospital in the name of behavior
modification. Although it is a fact that some psychotherapists
have misused behavior therapy methods in a dehumanizing way,
lending some credence to the common perception, many of the
labels are clearly exaggerated, if not downright erroneous. They
rest on several serious misunderstandings.

1. "Behavior therapy is deterministic: it teaches people to be
robots."

Behavior therapy is indeed based on the theory of determinism, a theory which asserts that everything we do has a cause.
Nothing happens without a reason. If this were not so, human
behavior could not be studied and accurately predicted. Some
early behavior therapists did in fact describe humans as being
robotlike.

The deterministic position held by most behavior therapists
today, however, in no way portrays us as robots or automatons,
without thought or freedom, controlled in stimulus-response
fashion by our passions or past conditioning. Rather it holds that
nothing ever happens—not even a creative thought—without
preceding events, events which are not necessarily beyond an
individual's control. These prior events can be one's own pre-
paratory thoughts, daydreams, or visions that precede and lay
the groundwork for the creative thought. They can be theological
beliefs, one's rearing as a child, earlier choices, ingrained habits,
or cultural mores. The reader who has difficulty accepting this
position, sometimes called soft determinism, might at least con-

sider adopting it as a working hypothesis, accepting it tempo-
rarily while practicing behavioral modes of counseling. As I see
it, most modes of counseling, even the more traditional ones,
are also dependent on this philosophical position.

In behavior therapy this elementary principle is used to explain
why people do what they do: behavior must be cued, or stim-
ulated, and it must be maintained. The stimulus or cue for a
behavior may be anything from the sound of an alarm clock
(for rousing one out of bed) to the smell of popcorn (for stim-
ulating a person to eat). Maintenance of behavior goes a step
further; although given many names (such as "the pleasure principle" or "reinforcement"), it essentially means that people tend
to do more frequently that which brings positive results or
pleasure, and less frequently that which brings negative conse-
quences or pain. Therefore a person who is lucky at fishing, has
fun hooking a fish, and enjoys eating fresh fish crisply fried will
be more likely to go on repeated fishing trips than the person
who hates the cold night air and mosquitoes, can't seem to land
a fish, and doesn't particularly enjoy eating fish anyway.

Behavioral methods rely on the identification and use of cues
and reinforcers. They assume prior and even causal factors in
human behavior, but they do not require a hard determinism that
would dehumanize persons.

2. "Behavior therapy is the same as behavior modification."

Actually, behavior therapy is *not* synonymous with behavior
modification, and especially not with behavior modification's
distortions and extremes: electric shock therapy, prefrontal
lobotomy, and other phenomena, real and surreal, used (or
thought to be used) in prisons and mental hospitals. While behavior therapy is indeed one form of behavior modification, *all*
therapies—Gestalt, client-centered, analytical—are also forms
of behavior modification in the sense that they all work towards
the eventual modification or changing of behavior.

3. "Behavior therapy is superficial or simplistic."

Behavior therapy is sometimes said to ignore the deep-seated,
underlying causes of a person's problems. The impression is that
a behavior therapist is concerned only about external events and

ignores such inner-world phenomena as feelings and thoughts. This view mistakenly assumes that one must always get to these "deeper" things before treatment can occur.

As already mentioned, behavior therapy deals with both kinds of behavior, the overt or observable and the covert or inner. But evidence from recent research belies the opinion of most traditional therapies that early childhood experiences must be known before a problem can be treated. These early experiences are frequently not significant in the development of the problem, nor is their discovery necessary for treatment. It is not always required that we know the circumstances surrounding the earliest onset of the problem.* Effective treatment of a woman's obesity may not require knowing her deep-seated unresolved feelings about her mother or even raising her low self-esteem; it may simply be a matter of helping her to monitor and perhaps permanently to change some of her eating habits, for example, by bringing no more high-calorie snacks into the house or by eating only at the table and only at regular mealtimes. The obesity has its original causes, of course, but these generally do not have to be "worked through," nor does she necessarily have to know about them in order for her to deal effectively with her weight problem. Behavioral methods do not espouse superficiality, but neither do they shun quick and direct approaches to the problem of immediate concern.

4. "Behavior therapy will result in 'symptom substitution'."

Researchers indicate that persons in behavior therapy rarely develop new symptoms. The phenomenon of "symptom substitution"—the formation of another problem to replace the one being treated—is not unknown. Fear of its occurrence, however, is far more common than the reality itself. Behavioral methods can be highly effective and permanently effective in dealing with symptoms rather than in simply shuffling them about.

5. "Behavior therapy is akin to brainwashing or coercion."

A common criticism of behavior therapy is that it controls people. Unquestionably, human beings are susceptible to brainwashing. Cases of abuse by political and religious cults are picked up quickly by the press—but they have nothing to do with behavior therapy. The goal of behavior therapy is not to control the client but to help the client develop self-control. The very fact that a parishioner comes to the pastor for help is an admission than a portion of that person's life is out of control. The task of the pastoral counselor using behavioral methods is to train the person in the skills necessary for regaining self-control.

Unlike therapies that may foster dependency on the counselor, behavior therapy nurtures a person's independence from the very outset. It treats the person as a mature individual. Through collaboration, counselor and client together agree on the desired goals and the ways of reaching them. To be sure, the counselor is mainly responsible for choosing the means, but the client ordinarily states the goals, except of course in the case of severely depressed, psychotic, or autistic individuals who cannot make their own assessments or choices—extreme cases which are not dealt with in this book. Ordinarily, the counselees determine what they want to change. If the counselor were to choose the goals, behavior therapy could indeed be coercive. Brainwashing and behavior therapy may be similar in drawing upon the information gleaned from behavioral research, but there the similarity ends. In legitimate behavior therapy the ends are chosen by the counselee, while in brainwashing they are not.

Behavioral methods do not violate but strengthen the self. They do not bypass or short circuit but directly appeal to the personal center and its mature independence. Pastors considering these helpful modalities need to check carefully their prior conceptions and not embrace uncritically the many common misunderstandings.

What Changes Occur in Counseling?

It is certainly not my contention that behavior therapy is the end-all of counseling methods. It is simply one more tool, and a good one. Indeed, for me it has become the single most effective counseling approach for the widest variety of everyday problems, from the most bizarre to the most common situations a pastor will face. It produces change.

Actually, there are three major areas on which a counselor can focus in the attempt to bring change: feelings, thoughts or cognitions (including beliefs), and overt behaviors. Most traditional therapies have operated mainly in the first area, focusing primarily on changing feelings or emotions. Approaches such as the rational-emotive therapy (RET) of Albert Ellis have worked mainly in the second area, to alter cognitions, or thoughts and beliefs.* In the third area, the early pioneers in behavior therapy concentrated almost exclusively on bringing change in overt behavior. More recently, as I have noted, behavior therapy focuses on cognition (which determines feelings) as well as action. Thus all three categories are encompassed in the meaning of the word *behavior* in present-day behavior therapy.† The behavior therapist today is concerned also with feelings, but more at the point of assessment and as byproducts of cognitive and behavioral change, rather than for purposes of attacking them directly, as a Freudian therapist might. For the Freudian, feelings are the primary data to be considered. Behaviorists believe differently; feeling is merely one of many covert behaviors.

Most of the counseling situations in which a parish pastor can effect change are short-term or crisis in nature. In such instances behavioral methods will often prove best suited for starting to effect change, while methods aimed at altering emotions may best be used later. The wise and compassionate pastor will use whatever change-provoking methods are propitious in a given situation, whether they aim at changing feelings, or thoughts, or overt behaviors. Pastors who counsel from a theological perspective and within the context of a supporting community will be cautious about uncritically adopting ideologies that may be at variance with their faith, but neither will they be misled by stereotypes or misunderstandings into neglecting counseling approaches which can effect change, thereby bringing relief and hope to all the Raymond Carlsons they seek to serve.

2. Helping People Cope with Stress

Imagine for a moment that you are a Cro-Magnon man or woman, strolling down your favorite jungle path in search of some hairy mammoth for supper. The sun is shining, the sky is blue, and it is a great day to be out hunting. All of a sudden, as you round a bend, there stands a ferocious Tyrannosaurus rex, licking its chops. Instantly you realize that instead of bagging a meal, you may soon become one. Your whole system reacts immediately to the threat. Blood flows to the control areas of your body, adrenalin pumps into your blood, giving you the strength to act. Your heartbeat accelerates, your muscles tense, you are ready either to tangle with the beast or to hightail it out of there. Since you don't own a rifle and you left your best spear in the hall closet, and the other creature weighs eight metric tons, your brain makes a microsecond decision to do the 440-yard dash, and you are off, beating a rapid retreat to shelter.

Now imagine yourself on the Hollywood Freeway at rush hour, driving in the fast lefthand lane, trying to make it home ahead of the guests you have invited for dinner. All of a sudden a Chevy pickup in the lane next to yours starts to move over—to where you are! Instantly you see the danger. Your body reacts with increased heartbeat and adrenalin, just as in your jungle hunting expedition. You hit the brakes hard, swerve to the left as much as you can, and mutter a few "expletives deleted."

What is so marvelous about the creation of our bodies is that this fight-or-flight response, our instant reaction to danger, occurs whether the peril is Tyrannosaurus rex, a Chevy pickup, a call from the school principal about your child, or word from the church council that the pastor's salary will not be raised next year. But a difference exists between how we handled these fight-or-flight situations eons ago in the jungle and how we handle them now. Then we "had at it" with the beast or took a short-cut back to the cave; either way, we used up the adrenalin in our blood, exercised our muscles until they ached, and after-wards collapsed in exhaustion. On the freeway our hearts may pound for a while, the veins in our foreheads may throb for a time, but we have not exercised our muscles or quickly burned up the adrenalin.

As dangers, threats, and stresses multiply in our lives today, our bodies have a tendency to remain in a low-level state of arousal, constantly ready for action. This keyed-up state is what we often refer to as anxiety or tension. Instead of feeling the good exhaustion that follows vigorous exercise, we feel drained, find our stomach in knots, experience tension headaches, and have trouble getting to sleep at night. Or we may become too quick on the draw with the church council. Instead of being able to fight or flee as our distant ancestors did, we live with the anxiety-creating situations, seeking "escape" through popping Valium, drinking beer, or burying ourselves in TV. For many of us in today's hectic society, anxiety is a constant, a way of life. But there are ways of handling it more appropriately.

A Case of Anxiety

Janice Winters was not drinking excessively like a friend of hers, but she knew she had to do something when her dentist declared her a tooth grinder and hinted that maybe she needed to see somebody about it because "it could be emotional." It was; Janice had known for some time that something was wrong, but she had been afraid to face it. Besides, she was so busy. In fact, that was part of her problem.

Matt, her husband, had decided after seven years in the Navy that he did not want to make a career of it. Matt returned to college and Janice had to go to work. It was hard for both of them—and for their two preschool children. Matt was studying constantly, it seemed, plus working almost full time. Janice served as secretary for a "tyrant." She detested working in an office, but "It's all I can do and, besides, the pay is okay." Most of all she hated sending her two daughters to nursery school. She had always thought that "a mother should be at home when her children are young." She felt guilty.

Janice was on edge all the time. She had trouble sleeping. She

was taking both tranquilizers and sleeping medication as prescribed by her doctor. She hated using them but saw no way out.
She was also on medication for her frequent tension headaches.

Janice was not exactly at the end of her rope, but she knew
it was time to do something. Her first thought was of Henry
Beyers. Although she had been critical of him in the past for
doing too much counseling and not enough of his "churchly
duties," she knew that her pastor was a good counselor. One of
her friends in the adult class had assured her of that.

As Janice and Pastor Beyers reviewed her different problems,
they surfaced a number of items potentially related to anxiety.
She would grind her teeth (ruining her dental work), she experienced tension headaches, she had problems getting to sleep and
felt fatigued all the time. Emotionally, she felt pressure from all
sides, guilt about leaving her children in the care of others, and
lack of support from her husband.

Three behavioral approaches were used in Janice's case. First,
Pastor Beyers worked with her on the matter of thinking about
certain things. Together they tried to clarify her cognitions (cognitive therapy will be discussed in the next chapter). The pastor
thereby helped her deal with her feelings of guilt and anxiety
about her daughters. He shared recent research findings which
revealed that in certain respects children are actually better off
in child care centers than at home, that in the group situation
they progress faster and develop more skill in learning and in
interpersonal relationships than do children who are raised exclusively in their own home.

In the second place, Janice and her pastor together problem-
solved the situation, finding ways in which she could simplify her
life and cut some potentially stress-producing stimuli (problem
solving will be discussed in chapter 5). Janice was committed to
helping her husband in his education, but Pastor Beyers also
suggested that she find ways to "do something for Janice." She
decided to trade babysitting chores with a neighbor so that she
and her husband could enjoy an occasional weekend alone,
camping in the mountains, and she guessed she might afford one
nice restaurant lunch a week with her co-workers at the office.
She even started thinking about taking her turn at a college
education within a year or so.

But the immediate problem was still that Janice had too much anxiety. Pastor Beyers believed that a third approach, training in relaxation, could be helpful, and most of the counseling time was spent in this way. Janice had belonged to an early morning prayer group in the church before Matt left the Navy. She dropped it when she went back to work. Pastor Beyers had recently been using some autogenic exercise (described later in this chapter) with the prayer group to help them relax and to assist them in focusing their thoughts. The pastor suggested that Janice rejoin the group and renew her daily devotional life at a prearranged time each morning while her husband took responsibility for the children; at this time she was to practice her autogenic exercises.

The pastor led her through relaxation exercises during their third session together, and she recorded his words on a cassette tape recorder. Janice was an "easy learner" and got quickly into the exercises and daily devotions at home. She noticed the change immediately in her sleeping. At her next session she reported jubilantly: "I've had my first good night's sleep since I returned to work." It took a bit longer for her to discern any effect on her headaches, and at least four weeks went by before their frequency had greatly diminished. Even after the counseling was terminated, whenever she became tense she recognized it first in the form of a headache. This is one of the benefits of relaxation training: you develop a sensitivity to your body, which frequently signals that something is wrong before you are aware of the problem cognitively.

Relaxation Training

How do you go about training someone to relax? Most of us have had the experience of consciously trying to calm down and only ending up more upset, more tense than before. If Pastor Beyers had advised "just relaxing" for Janice, it is possible that her inability to relax would have become an additional frustration and led to even greater tension and anxiety.

It has been shown from both a medical and a psychological point of view that, for some people, learning physical relaxation is helpful in reducing emotional stress. With the addition of some cognitive procedures such as those noted in the next chapter, these relaxation methods can be even more beneficial.

The human brain has a feedback system which includes tension sensors in the muscle cells which signal the muscles to tense for action when fear triggers the need (such as the cave dweller's chance meeting with Tyrannosaurus rex, or the freeway driver's encounter with the Chevy pickup). Unfortunately, in most situations arising in our modern society muscular action is not what is usually needed. When the anxiety and muscle tension are prolonged, the control center in the brain becomes set, like a thermostat, to higher and higher levels of tolerable muscle tension; the increased tension of the muscles can keep the mind apprehensive, and the apprehension in turn triggers increased muscle tension. The vicious cycle can be broken at either end: psychotherapy (focusing especially on how we *think* about certain potentially anxiety-provoking situations—see the next chapter) can result in reduced muscle tension and, conversely, relaxation therapy (which focuses on the muscles) can relieve the anxiety. Ideally, effective pastoral counseling will do both. The minister will train parishioners in relaxation methods while also helping them to think differently and within their environments to make different choices so as to reduce the potential for stress.

Methods of Relaxation

Anxious individuals can be trained to relax, and there are a number of ways for doing this: progressive muscle relaxation, autogenic training, biofeedback, hypnosis and self-hypnosis, yoga, Transcendental Meditation, heart-lung exercise (through jogging, for example), meditation, and prayer. Some of these methods are only marginally helpful, but others are easily adaptable to the pastor's work, as we shall see in the following pages. We begin with a description of two methods of relaxation training.

Progressive Relaxation

The first method, progressive relaxation, was first developed in the 1930s by Edmund Jacobson, a physician at the University of Chicago.* Although generally known, the method was not practiced extensively until the fifties, when Joseph Wolpe adapted it for his systematic desensitization behavior therapy.†

What follows here is a transcript of a progressive relaxation

79731   254.5
S877

Brescia College Library

Owensboro, Kentucky

method I have used for reducing muscle tension.* The words
are those of the counselor:

Let your eyelids be lightly closed or partially open. Adopt
a let-it-happen, passive attitude and let relaxation occur at its
own pace. If your mind wanders off to other thoughts, don't
worry; gently let them pass by and calmly come back to doing
the exercise.

Now become aware of your body. Scan over it. Notice how
it feels.

Now become aware of your right arm and hand. Notice how
they feel. Keeping the other muscles of your body relaxed,
extend your right arm straight out in front of you while pulling your hand back at the wrist. Hold it. (Hold five to seven
seconds in this and the following segments.) / Sense the
tension building. . . . Now relax your hand, lower your arm
while imagining and feeling the tension flowing out and the
relaxation flowing in. Let your arm and hand be loose and
limp, heavy and relaxed. Feel the relaxation.

Now shift your attention to your left arm and hand. Notice
how they feel. Keeping the other muscles of your body relaxed, extend your left arm straight out in front of you while
pulling your hand back at the wrist. Hold it. / Sense the
tension building. . . . Now relax your hand, lower your arm
while imagining and feeling the tension flowing out and the
relaxation flowing in. Let your arm and hand be loose and
limp, heavy and relaxed. Feel the relaxation.

Now become aware of both your arms and hands. Notice
how they feel. Keeping the other muscles of your body relaxed, extend both arms straight out in front of you. Now
make a tight fist with both hands. Hold it. / Sense the tension
building. . . . Now relax your hands, lower your arms while
imagining and feeling the tension flowing out and the relaxation flowing in. Let your arms and hands be loose and limp,
heavy and relaxed. Feel the relaxation.

Now shift your attention to your right leg and foot. Notice
how they feel. Keeping the other muscles of your body
relaxed, extend your right leg straight out in front of you and
pull your right foot and toes back towards you. Hold it. /

Sense the tension building. . . . Now relax your right foot and toes, lower your leg while imagining and feeling the tension flowing out and the relaxation flowing in. Let your right leg and foot be loose and limp, heavy and relaxed. Feel the relaxation.

Now become aware of your left leg and foot. Notice how they feel. Keeping the other muscles of your body relaxed, extend your left leg straight out in front of you and pull your left foot and toes back towards you. Hold it. / Sense the tension building. . . . Now relax your left foot and toes, lower your leg while imagining and feeling the tension flowing out and the relaxation flowing in. Let your left leg and foot be loose and limp, heavy and relaxed. Feel the relaxation.

Now shift your attention to both your legs and feet. Notice how they feel. Keeping the other muscles of your body relaxed, extend both legs straight out in front of you while pressing your feet and toes forward. Hold it. / Sense the tension building. . . . Now relax your feet and toes, lower your feet and legs while imagining and feeling the tension flowing out and the relaxation flowing in. Let your legs and feet be loose and limp, heavy and relaxed. Feel the relaxation.

Now become aware of your chest and abdomen. Notice how they feel. Keeping the other muscles of your body relaxed, pull your abdomen in tightly and expand your chest. Hold it. / Sense the tension building. . . . Now relax your abdomen and chest while imagining and feeling the tension flowing out and the relaxation flowing in. Let your chest and abdomen be loose and limp, heavy and relaxed. Feel the relaxation.

Now shift your attention to your back. Notice how it feels. Keeping the other muscles of your body relaxed and your breathing calm and regular, pull your shoulders straight back while gently arching your upper back backwards, allowing your abdomen and pelvis to go forward. Hold it. / Feel the tension building. . . . Now relax your back while imagining and feeling the tension flowing out and the relaxation flowing in. Let your entire back be loose and limp, heavy and relaxed. Feel the relaxation.

Now shift your attention to your shoulders, neck, and face. Notice how they feel. Keeping the other muscles of your body relaxed, raise your shoulders up towards your ears, keeping your lower arms relaxed, and gently press your head backwards while biting your jaws tightly together and squeezing your eyelids closed. Hold it but keep breathing. / Feel the tension building. . . . Now lower your shoulders, relax your neck, jaws, and eyes and your entire face, while imagining and feeling the tension flowing out and the relaxation flowing in. Let your shoulders and neck be loose and limp, heavy and relaxed, your jaw loose and slack, your eyes relaxed and calm, and your entire face soft and relaxed, cool and calm. Feel the relaxation in your shoulders, neck, and face.

Now scan over your entire body and sense the good feelings of relaxation that exist in your mind and body.

Now I'm going to count, slowly, from one to five. At the count of five, take a deep breath. On the inhale say, "Mind alert, wide awake, open your eyes widely." On the exhale say, "Relaxed and refreshed." One. Coming up. Two. Three. Four. Five. Breathe in deeply. Say, "Mind alert, wide awake, open your eyes widely." Exhale saying, "Relaxed and refreshed." Gently stretch all your muscles, then slowly get up, feeling alert and refreshed.

It should be noted that the effective use of progressive relaxation requires variation and individualization for each counselee, taking into consideration the special needs or physical conditions (for example, the back trouble or neck trouble) of that particular person. It is critical that in the period of five to seven seconds during which the muscles are held tense, they should be quite tight but never to the point of pain. It is likely that in the beginning not all parts of the body can be covered, but as practice sharpens skill in progressive relaxation techniques, the client can add further areas of the body.

Autogenic Exercises

A second method of relaxation, autogenic training, was developed by Schultz and Luthe. Although it is not hypnosis, it is based on hypnosis research. It trains clients to relax muscles not through physical exercises, as in progressive relaxation, but by mental control. As with progressive relaxation, most clients will probably not be able to do all areas of the body during the first practice. The transcript follows.*

Let your eyelids be lightly closed or partially open. Adopt a let-it-happen, passive attitude and let relaxation occur at its own pace.

Become aware of your body. Scan over it. Notice how it feels. Take several deep breaths and allow your whole body to relax.

Now just let your breathing be natural, calm, and regular. Stay a passive observer of your environment but label whatever comes into your awareness. If it is a sound you hear, mentally say "sound." If it is a feeling you feel, say "feeling." If you are thinking about a memory, say "memory." If it is a fantasy, say "fantasy." Just do this for the next minute. /

Now imagine yourself alone, lying on a warm, sunny beach, or floating on an air mattress in a backyard pool, or taking a hot bath, or in any other warm and relaxing situation. Just see yourself lying there, calm, warm, and comfortable, without a care in the world. Feel the relaxation.

Now become aware of your right arm and hand. Each time you exhale, mentally say, "My right arm is heavy (relaxed) and warm." Imagine warmth flowing down your arm, into your hand, and all the way to your fingertips. Allow your breathing to be calm and regular. Now just let your right arm and hand be loose and limp, warm and relaxed. Feel the warmth and relaxation.

Now shift your attention to your left arm and hand. Each time you exhale, mentally say, "My left arm is heavy (relaxed) and warm." Imagine warmth flowing down your arm, into your hand, and all the way to your fingertips. Allow your breathing to be calm and regular. Now just let your left arm and hand be loose and limp, warm and relaxed. Feel the warmth and relaxation.

Now become aware of your right leg and foot. Each time you exhale, mentally say, "My right leg and foot are heavy (relaxed) and warm." Imagine warmth flowing down your leg and into your foot. Allow your breathing to be calm and regular. Now just let your right leg and foot be loose and limp, warm and relaxed. Feel the warmth and relaxation.

Now shift your attention to your left leg and foot. Each time you exhale, mentally say, "My left leg and foot are heavy (relaxed) and warm." Imagine warmth flowing down your leg and into your foot. Allow your breathing to be calm and regular. Now just let your left leg and foot be loose and limp, warm and relaxed. Feel the warmth and relaxation.

Now become aware of your heartbeat. Each time you exhale, mentally say, "My heartbeat is calm and regular." Imagine your heartbeat relaxed, calm, and regular.

Now place your hand on your upper abdomen. Each time you exhale, mentally say, "My abdomen (solar plexus) is warm." Imagine warmth flowing into your abdomen. Feel the warmth and relaxation.

Now just let your entire body be warm and relaxed, your mind calm and quiet. Let your breathing continue to be calm and regular, and just enjoy the good, healthy sense of relaxation that now exists in your mind and body. While doing this, mentally say, "I am . . ." as you inhale and ". . . relaxed (calm)" as you exhale.

Now I'm going to count, slowly, from one to five. At the count of five, take a deep breath. On the inhale say, "Mind alert, wide awake, open your eyes widely." On the exhale say, "Relaxed and refreshed." One. Coming up. Two. Three. Four. Five. Breathe in deeply. Say, "Mind alert, wide awake, open your eyes widely." Exhale saying, "Relaxed and refreshed." Gently stretch all your muscles, then slowly get up, feeling alert and refreshed.

Relaxation Methods in Pastoral Counseling

Progressive relaxation and autogenic training can both be used to good effect in pastoral counseling. Following are some suggestions for enhancing that effectiveness:

(1) The physical surroundings in which the client practices relaxation training, whether at home or in the pastor's study, must be conducive to relaxation. The place should be quiet and

free of interruptions, illuminated with a low, gentle light. If out-side noise (a pounding typewriter or ringing telephone) is a problem, install a white-sound protector (available from com-panies supplying psychological therapeutic equipment) or sim-ply turn on the fan in the heater or air conditioner and let it run continuously to provide a steady background hum. No office phone or intercom should ring. The temperature in the room needs to be made comfortable, possibly a degree or two warmer than usual. It is important, especially for autogenic training, that the person not be cold.

Clients are asked to wear loose clothing or loosen their gar-ments a bit; it is suggested that girdles and other tight garments not be worn during practice sessions. Occasionally clients may wish to keep their eyes open until they are comfortable enough to close them; Individuals who wear contact lenses will want to remove them. People practicing relaxation should either sit or recline on a firm bed, couch, or comfortable chair. My clients seem to prefer a comfortable recliner for both relaxation training and verbal counseling; I urge them to move around in the chair or couch only as much as needed to be comfortable.

(2) The purpose and possible benefits of relaxation training have to be thoroughly explained before beginning. This is im-portant. If clients do not understand or approve of the effort, if they fight the process, it will not succeed.

They will have to practice once or twice a day for about fifteen minutes until they learn to relax rapidly. It is preferable that one session be in the morning, soon after the trainees have awakened, and one in the evening. If they don't practice regu-larly, they will not learn the skill. Part of the therapy contract, discussed in the previous chapter, can include relaxation train-ing and writing down the results of each practice session. A sim-ple chart may be helpful in recording the results:*

0	25	50	75	100
No tension; completely relaxed	Very relaxed		Very tense	No relaxa-tion; maxi-mum tension

(3) Trainees are told they are learning a skill—nothing magical—much like learning to drive a car. The difference is that they are not to *try* in the way they usually try to learn a new skill, but, on the contrary, they are to develop a passive attitude. They are to will themselves to relax but not "force it" and not be upset if it doesn't happen right away. This is extremely important. "Not trying" can be upsetting to some trainees who fear losing control; the repeated question about how they are feeling can help elicit the expression of such reactions. I explain to trainees that they actually are in control: what is needed for relaxation is a passive self-control which allows the muscles to relax themselves.

(4) Before beginning relaxation practice, a physical examination by the person's own doctor may be advised. If clients have any doubts about their medical readiness, or in the cases of progressive relaxation if they are susceptible to muscle spasms or back or knee problems, a physician should definitely be consulted.

(5) During the exercises some trainees will feel a floating sensation or a tingly or crawly feeling in fingers, arms, or legs. They may also feel uncomfortably warm. It is best to predict such possibilities before starting so that the people are not frightened by them if they occur.

(6) Frequently it is easier for clients to practice relaxation if they begin by using a cassette tape of the exercise. Tapes can be prepared in any of three ways: (*a*) transcripts of the above exercises can be prerecorded on tapes and given to clients at the first training sessions, (*b*) clients can bring a cassette tape recorder to the session and tape the exercises as the counselor leads the first practice, (*c*) prerecorded tapes available from various biofeedback therapists can be used.

Ultimately the parishioners will need to be weaned from the tapes and practice at their own pace from memory. When trainees feel that the tape is moving too slowly, now that they have learned to relax more rapidly, it is a sign that they do not need the tapes anymore. However, if at any future time they should feel uptight or develop difficulty in relaxing, they can go back to the tapes. It is beneficial to use the complete tape once a month as a booster shot reinforcing the full relaxation method.

(7) It is important that the counselor's speech during the practice session and on the tape be in a slow, fairly deep, calm, and relaxed voice—which means that the counselor too needs to be reasonably relaxed. There is nothing more fruitless than a tense counselor trying to train a tense client not to be tense. Failure will abound.

It is therefore necessary for counselors to practice for themselves all the relaxation methods they plan to use, before they begin administering them to clients in actual counseling. Until these methods have been used for quite a while, the minister should probably practice along with the counselee. This helps to improve timing and to increase sensitivity throughout the process.

Advanced Relaxation Methods

The slow, step-by-step process described above seems necessary in the early stages of training, while the person is learning to relax. Once the basic steps have been learned, however, more advanced methods may be used to generalize the learning, apply it more extensively to daily life, and shorten the time needed to achieve relaxation. Space here does not allow for a full explanation of these methods, but a brief description of at least a few of them may be helpful.

One advanced exercise, requiring only one to two minutes, is especially helpful to those clients who relax best with the progressive relaxation method. It involves tensing as many of the body muscles as possible all at once. Clients are instructed to stand on their tiptoes, clench their fists, scrunch up their faces, raise their shoulders, and tip their heads back. They are also to tighten as many other muscle groups as possible for five to seven seconds. This is followed by fifteen seconds of letting all muscles go limp and then sensing the feeling of relaxation after releasing them. The method is best when used twice in succession.

A second advanced method that takes only a few minutes involves having the counselees close their eyes and monitor their breathing for a minute, focusing on the exhale. Then they are instructed to say at each inhale, "I am . . ." and at each exhale, ". . . letting go." This is to be done for one to two minutes.

Another advanced method involves asking clients to sit calmly and, after initially relaxing through use of one of the two basic methods, close their eyes and focus the exhaling of breath through the nose, repeating on each exhale the word *calm* or *relax*. By continuing to do this, the pairing of relaxation with the words *calm* or *relax* is reinforced. Then, in the future, the repetition of these words at tense moments in a busy day can actually bring relaxation.

Yet another technique has the clients begin by using one of the two basic methods to begin relaxation and then visualize any relaxing place or event, one that is calculated to calm rather than excite. For example: "See yourself floating in an inflatable raft on a quiet, sunny lake. Feel the warmth of the sun baking on your skin, the smell of the lake, the sound of the wind blowing through the pine trees on shore. Let your imagination go and allow all of your senses to become alive. Allow yourself to totally relax in this situation."

One additional mode of advanced relaxation training involves coupling any form of relaxation practice with a morning (or evening) devotional time. The two benefit and complement each other. Specific meditation techniques (such as Transcendental Meditation) can be coupled with this devotional time if clients want to use them.

Relaxation helps people arrive at that openness and patient waiting which is necessary for the word of God to be heard. This open, quiet waiting in turn deepens the body's relaxation. Your fourth grade Sunday school teacher was right when she spoke about your need for a private devotional life. It probably never entered her mind that such a quiet time was also good for the treatment of anxiety!

Some Additional Helps: Biofeedback

There is still more help available in training people to relax. Most of us by now have either heard of biofeedback or read about it in newspapers or magazines. It has been the news story of the past few years in the mental health field. Biofeedback's benefits have been touted, and many "experts" in the technique have come out of the woodwork. Some of what they claim is true, much not. A few leaders have been genuinely ahead of their time; others are charlatans in search of money or fame.

Biofeedback is simply the process of providing an organism—
even a human being—with immediate information about a certain bodily response such as heartbeat or skin temperature so
that, given an awareness of that response, the organism can learn
to adjust or change in the light of it. One purpose of the bodily
feedback can be to aid in more effective relaxation.

There is nothing new, unusual, or magical about biofeedback.
You have probably used at least one biofeedback device already
today—your bathroom mirror. Each time you glance at a mirror
you find out something about yourself that you would not have
known had you not glanced at it. The mirror lets you know how
you look, but it does not change your appearance. Only you can
do that.

The same principle is involved in biofeedback. The equipment
used, however, is obviously more complex than a mirror. Biofeedback uses accurate electronic sensors, placed on the skin,
which pick up and amplify various body functions and immediately display them for the trainee by means of sound, meters, or
lights. The most commonly measured items are muscle tenseness,
skin temperature, and the electrical activity of the skin. Some
biofeedback therapists measure brain waves, but unless their
equipment is highly sophisticated it will be unable to reject spuri-
ous output and will therefore be ineffective.

The two pieces of equipment most beneficial for biofeedback
training are the EMG (electromyograph) and the temperature
sensor. The EMG measures the tension level in certain skeletal
muscles and reports on it visually or audibly. Trainees learn to
relax these muscles with some of the exercises involved in the
two basic relaxation methods described above, using the immediate feedback flashed on the meter or heard in the tone signal
to measure the success of their efforts.

The other piece of equipment, the temperature sensor or
trainer, is likely to be more useful to the pastoral counselor. It
measures skin temperature and is used for gauging blood flow.
Easy to use and relatively inexpensive, it is nothing more than
a highly accurate electronic thermometer, taped usually to a
fingertip. As a part of the fight-or-flight response referred to
above, during a stress situation blood goes to the central organs
of the body and the brain. It leaves the capillaries, and the

fingers get cold. (Recall how cold your hands were when you gave your first sermon in front of the homiletics professor and all of your classmates.) The clients' task is to raise the temperature in their fingertips.

Biofeedback can be helpful, and we have mentioned it in this chapter for one main reason: people often learn faster through using the equipment. A good biofeedback therapist can tell from the equipment's feedback what types of relaxation exercises work best with each individual; in my own case, for example, the feedback showed a greater amount of positive change with autogenic exercises than with progressive relaxation. Another advantage is that the equipment indicates positive movement in the direction of relaxation even before the person feels the change; it is an early "reward."

There is of course one drawback—biofeedback equipment is expensive for ministers to use. A minimally adequate EMG apparatus may cost many hundreds of dollars, and good equipment more than a thousand. As a compromise, the pastor may want to consider investing in a temperature trainer, described above; it is the easiest piece of equipment to use and probably the most beneficial for use at the beginning of relaxation training. An electonic thermometer, like those used by physicians, the temperature trainer is much less expensive. It reads out temperature in tenths of a degree and is small enough to fit in the palm of the hand.

In addition to the basic and advanced relaxation methods and biofeedback, referral is another important way of helping. Even though I am presently engaged in specialized full-time pastoral counseling, I prefer not to do most of my own relaxation training. Rather I refer people to a local biofeedback therapist who does it inexpensively. Indeed, I would suggest that pastors send counselees who could benefit from biofeedback to a qualified practitioner nearby. For however helpful it may be from an efficiency standpoint, biofeedback is not an indispensable necessity in pastoral counseling, even where relaxation training is being given.

When Are Relaxation Methods Beneficial?

What types of people can be helped by these relaxation techniques? The simple answer is: almost everyone who suffers from

anxiety in one form or another. Rathus and Nevid have listed
a number of the typical bodily sensations associated with anxiety,
sensations which might serve as a guide to the kinds of counseling cases that could best be helped by the methods discussed in
this chapter:*

—sensation of a tight band around the head
—heart beating rapidly, skipping beats, or beating irregularly
—stomach in knots
—trembling hands, arms, legs, voice
—dry mouth
—difficulty in breathing, feeling out of breath
—chest pains
—stiff or tight neck, arms, back of shoulders
—cold hands, feet
—numb hands, arms, legs
—weak hands, arms, legs, body
—difficulty in swallowing
—heavy sweating without exertion
—diarrhea
—dizziness, nausea, light-headedness, or fainting

People who will not benefit from relaxation training are those
individuals who for physical or mental reasons are not able to
practice the exercises. Since anxiety and relaxation are almost
always mutually exclusive, relaxation methods can be helpful in
the case of various ailments involving emotional or physical
tension. They can be helpful for persons suffering from such
psychosomatic disorders as migraine or tension headache, ulcers,
miscellaneous stomach ailments, lower back pain, or the symptoms listed above, particularly in cases which doctors have determined are caused by tension and are not physically based.
Relaxation methods can also be beneficial for tooth grinders and
insomniacs.

Relaxation therapy, besides relieving such ailments, is also
helpful for emotional and interpersonal problems where tension
exists. I have found it useful for people with phobias, large
amounts of anger, and high job tension. It has remarkably trans-
formed several homes in which the husband came home carrying
the tension and pressure of his job, and the wife, cooped up all

day with preschool children, was ready to pull her hair out by the time he arrived. Relaxation training prepared them to tolerate frustrations and cope better with the day's problems and to reenter the family relationship each evening with less bickering and greater opportunity for mutual understanding and support.

Relaxation is the counter to anxiety. People in distress who come for counseling can be taught the skills of relaxation. These skills not only lessen anxiety-related physical ailments and improve interpersonal relaitonships; they also foster an openness and a patient waiting which is beneficial in hearing the word spoken to us in our hectic lives.

3. Using Cognitive Methods in Pastoral Counseling

Your plane has landed, and you and your spouse are whisked to the hotel. For several months the two of you have planned on going to the annual church convention two days early and making it a short vacation. But now the desk clerk says he has no record of your reservation. He asks for your confirmation. You think you left it at your office. Asked if he has another room, the clerk says, "I'm sorry, but we are booked solid for the next three days. There is a golf tournament in town, and most of the rooms are taken for that."

Losing your usual calm composure, you become angry and start demanding a room. The desk clerk has handled such situations many times before and is implacable: "I'm sorry, but all our rooms are full, and I show no reservation for you." Nothing can be done. You explode, use some biblical terms in a way that is atypical for you, and storm out of the hotel. Thus begins the vacation time when you had hoped to leave the problems and pressures of life behind you.

After booking into a nice room in a nearby motel and after a hot shower and a good dinner, the Great Hotel Disaster doesn't seem so great or even a disaster. Later, meeting friends at the convention, you may complain about the incident and blame the hotel for ruining the first few hours of your vacation. But for now you don't dwell on it: there are three good days ahead, and you decide to relax and enjoy them.

The Apostle Paul speaks to such events in his Letter to the Philippians: "Not that I complain of want; for I have learned in whatever state I am, to be content" (Phil. 4:11). In this brief phrase, Paul shows the way to be happy regardless of external circumstances. Paul also makes it clear that this ability to be content is learned; it does not come naturally. Furthermore, he allows himself no exceptions: "in *whatever* state I am" (italics mine).

I believe that this passage—in fact the entire New Testament—speaks of how we ourselves bear responsibility for our own emotions and for what we say and do. Responsibility for my feelings does not rest with the hotel clerks of the world but with me. It is not the situation as such but how we choose to *think* about the situation that actually creates our feelings and actions. It is not because you can't get good help anymore that you are furious. It is not the hotel clerk who made you incensed. You caused your own anger. You alone are responsible for your angry words and actions. Your response to the situation is dictated not by the situation but by you, by your thinking about it, by your appraisal, cognition, and system of beliefs.

The Cognitive Roots of Emotion

Cognitively oriented behavior therapists believe that most, if not all, unadaptive emotions and behaviors are developed and maintained by cognitive factors, especially unrealistic expectations. Albert Ellis, one of the leaders in this area of behavior therapy, calls these unrealistic expectations "irrational beliefs."* According to Ellis and his school of rational-emotive therapy (RET), the emotional reaction comes last. What comes first is an activating event or experience (described in chapter 1 as a cue). Next comes the person's appraisal or interpretation of the activating event, ordinarily based on one's personal beliefs or theology. This leads finally to the emotional reaction or consequence. If, for example, you are angry after being rebuffed by the hotel clerk, the rebuff itself is not the cause of your anger; the real cause is your own thoughts about being rebuffed, perhaps your belief that the hotel clerk has no right to rebuff you and that you have every right to be treated with special respect and consideration—all of which could be irrational beliefs.

The case of Thelma Rhodes illustrates some of the ethical concerns at stake in any attack on a person's irrational belief systems. A religious social worker intensely active in the women's movement, Thelma was acutely aware—in her own life as well as in the lives of other women—of the injustices meted out to women by our male-dominated culture. Unfortunately, her passionate involvement in the cause of women's rights, and her upsetness over the manifest injustice, was taking its toll on her body.

Thelma was angry much of the time. She experienced painful stomach ailments. She reported having gone to two therapists before, both of whom happened to be professionals as upset about the inequities of the sexist system as she was. Her sessions with them tended to lapse into mutual blaming and emotional catharsis, which gave Thelma brief but not lasting relief. Her stomach problems finally reached the point where her physician indelicately declared, "Your stomach is eating you alive. See a shrink." Thelma's compromise was David Shuman, a man whom she at least knew and with whom she felt comfortable, her pastor.

Pastor Shuman recognized the difficulty faced in counseling Thelma: "The unfairness you are angry about is real enough." The task, as he saw it, was to teach her how to keep herself from getting upset, yet without sweeping the serious issues under the rug. Thelma expressed her concern: "If I'm not angry, doesn't that mean I'm knuckling under to a corrupt system?" Pastor Shuman shared his opinion that upsetness is not a quality or measure of commitment; in fact in many cases (as in Thelma's) it can cause immobilization and perhaps physical illness, thus taking the player out of the game. It should be noted that some people use anger as a constructive motivator towards positive change. In this sense anger can serve as a "contact emotion," drawing attention to issues that need changing. Constructive uses of anger are taught in assertiveness training, a behavioral method that cannot be treated within the limited confines of this book.*

After a thorough discussion of the ethical issues in front of them the pastor said to Thelma, "I can understand the anger you feel about the way male domination has hurt women, and your reluctance to give up that anger. But if you agree that being less upset will help rather than hinder, I believe I can help you learn to do it." Nearly immobilized already by her stomach pain, Thelma eagerly agreed.

In the next few sessions with Pastor Shuman, Thelma experienced "cognitive restructuring" (explained in the pages that follow). She unlearned certain irrational beliefs and unrealistic expectations and learned new ways of facing legitimate conflicts without upsetting herself over them.

By the time Ms. Rhodes was ready to terminate counseling on a regular basis, she was a changed person. Relaxed and confident, she was working with greatly increased effectiveness on the Women's Task Force of a major political party. Her stomach, though scarred, was no longer "eating her alive." She had discovered the wisdom of meeting her opponents on their level instead of unrealistically expecting them to be at the same state of raised consciousness that she had reached only after years of feminist involvement and concern. Educating them instead of quibbling with them, she learned, not only saved her nerves; it actually worked better! What is more, she discovered that there were other things in her life besides politics that she genuinely cared for: her mother and dad and younger sister, her intimate circle of friends, her interest in the theater, and a closeness with nature that had formerly been intense when she was a backpacking college student but had lately been missing. By relearning rational expectations and beliefs, Thelma was freed to become physically stronger, to lead a happier and more wellrounded life, and even to be a more effective agent of social change.

Irrational Beliefs

In the process of maturation and socialization in our culture, many people develop sets of beliefs that are indeed irrational. They are called irrational because they are not supported by the reality of our environment but function nonetheless with the power of religious convictions. Albert Ellis notes eleven of the irrational beliefs or ideas most common in our society:*

1. It is a dire necessity for an adult human being to be loved or approved by virtually every significant other in his or her community.
2. One should be thoroughly competent, adequate, and achieving in all possible respects if one is to consider oneself worthwhile.
3. Certain people are bad, wicked, or villainous and should be severely blamed and punished for their villainy.
4. It is awful—catastrophic—when things are not the way one would very much like them to be.

5. Human unhappiness is externally caused, and people have little or no ability to control their sorrows and disturbances.
6. If something is or may be dangerous or fearsome, one should be terribly concerned about it and should keep dwelling on the possibility of its occurring.
7. It is easier to avoid than to face certain difficulties and responsibilities in life.
8. One should be dependent on others; one needs someone stronger than oneself on whom to rely.
9. One's past history is an all-important determiner of one's present behavior, and because something once strongly affected one's life it should indefinitely have a similar effect.
10. One should become quite upset over other people's problems and disturbances.
11. There is invariably a right, precise, and perfect solution to human problems, and it is catastrophic if this perfect solution is not found.

Many upsetting emotional reactions and problem behaviors seen by the pastor arise because of an individual's implicit theology. Theologians are correct in criticizing the care and counseling done by pastors who do not concern themselves with the troubled person's theology or beliefs. When in the midst of a counseling session a depressed woman weeps because she feels "useless and not wanted," it may not be possible to come right out and tell her that she wouldn't be feeling depressed if she had the right beliefs; yet we have all seen cases where distortions of the Christian faith—a misunderstanding of the idea of sin or a fear of punishment by an angry God for some minor infraction—have caused problems in people's lives. Individuals' responses to many situations are determined by the way they *understand* the events, not by the events themselves.* Ellis believes that an unadaptive or upsetting emotional response arises from a person's indiscriminate and automatic labeling of a situation.† The extent to which a situation is labeled—identified—according to irrational ideas, such as those listed above, determines how extreme an unwanted emotion or action will be. It is unlikely that we purposely tell ourselves such irrational statements in real-life situations; what plagues us rather is the automatic generation of these detrimental beliefs.

Cognitive Restructuring

Most of you recall the late evening rap sessions at seminary where various sides of consubstantiation or premillenialism were hotly argued. Do you remember how many of your classmates changed their viewpoint as a result of the discussion? I surely don't recall changing many of my colleagues' beliefs. And I don't think it was because I was a poor debater. We simply didn't convince each other—and probably didn't expect to.

Changing unconstructive belief systems is not easy. It requires considerable counseling finesse. Yet ministers, because of their training in both counseling and belief systems, are in an ideal position among all the helping professionals for enabling people to rid themselves of irrational ideas.

Cognitive restructuring is a name given to the process of helping individuals to discard irrational beliefs and unrealistic expectations and assisting them to view situations more realistically. Much rational restructuring is akin historically to the educating of the laity in a correct theology. The church has always recognized—though recent pastoral counseling practice often has not—that our beliefs about self, others, the world, and God greatly affect how we act. The cognitive therapists also recognize this, but they refer to it in nontheological terms.

Gail Rayburn was making a pastoral call in the hospital. Visiting a member of her congregation who had undergone minor surgery, she was told by her parishioner, "Please stop for a few minutes and see the man next to me. He is very despondent and tried to end his life." Pastor Rayburn acted promptly on the suggestion. She spent only a few minutes with Donald Claymore, but to her surprise he called her by phone a week later and said he had to see her.

Upon entering Pastor Rayburn's office Donald, a twenty-nine-year-old draftsman, told of his wife leaving him to marry another man. He felt totally lost without her and had indeed attempted suicide: "I wouldn't do that again, though. I feel horrible about her leaving, but I don't want to go through *that* again."

Donald was shy and had dated only one other woman in his life. He demanded so much of himself that he believed no one—especially a woman—would ever want to talk to him, let alone spend an evening with him. Cognitive restructuring seemed in order.

Assessment

The first task Donald and the pastor faced in cognitive restructuring was that of assessment. Together they had to determine which irrational beliefs were troubling him. Pastor Rayburn, after explaining how irrational thoughts can cause our problem feelings and actions, asked Donald to read Ellis's book, *A New Guide to Rational Living*.

As we see in Donald Claymore's case, once an empathetic counseling relationship is established, the first task in cognitively oriented behavior therapy—as well as all other behavior therapies—is assessment. This task is best done by the counselees themselves, as explained in chapter 1. I like to send clients home to read a book or portion of a book.* I say to them, "You diagnose yourself. Read this, assess your life, and determine which irrational ideas are plaguing you. It may not be easy to admit some of these irrational beliefs. In fact, it can be downright embarrassing. But the more honest you allow yourself to be, the faster we can resolve your problems."

In Donald's case, he returned the next week and, referring to the Ellis list of eleven irrational ideas, noted, "I've got 1, 2, 4, 5, and 7." After some conversation, Pastor Rayburn suggested that Donald may also be troubled by number 8. He admitted the possibility: "I thought of it, but it's hard for a man to admit he might be dependent. I thought maybe it was because I was shy."

Teaching/Learning

After the initial assessment process, where clients begin to understand how they are upsetting themselves (explained in Ellis's RET theory†) and what irrational beliefs are causing their problems (reviewing the eleven irrational beliefs), the task is to help them change these beliefs. This is the heart of cognitive restructuring. With some individuals it is a simple process requiring only a few sessions; with others it is an arduous task and may even require that the pastor refer them to full-time counselors or agencies. In Donald's situation, he was hurting a great deal and was quite willing to face his irrational beliefs squarely.

Various methods of cognitive restructuring are available. In some cases one method may suffice; in others your creativity will be exhausted in matching resources to needs. A rational-emotive therapist like Ellis might confront and directly challenge the clients' irrational beliefs until they come around to a more realistic view of the world. Such a rational-emotive therapy session can be quite explosive, with therapist and client at times coming to verbal blows. This kind of confrontation needs to be used with considerable sensitivity.* Once a good rapport has been developed, more and more confrontation and challenging can be used without detrimental results as the counseling progresses.

Donald's self-confidence seemed a little tender for such a head-on approach. The best method for beginning cognitive restructuring with someone like him is to thoroughly explain the theory of rational-emotive therapy and review the eleven irrational beliefs. It is good to use numerous nontechnical examples to highlight your explanation. Illustrations may be drawn from some of the books listed in the Annotated Bibliography or, even better, from your own personal experiences or from the client's own life. Gail Rayburn hit upon an effective device in her work with Donald: "Think of two students taking an art class on sketching the human figure. While they are both working at their easels, the teacher circulates around the room, offering criticism to help the students do more effectively a very difficult task—drawing the human body. One student thinks to herself that she is glad this teacher offers plenty of criticism so that she can become a better artist. She also believes that the teacher's criticism shows interest in her work. The other student starts to worry when the instructor comes near him. He thinks the teacher is too critical and should tell students only positive things to encourage them. Now—since the professor is giving criticism equally to all the students, what is the difference between the two?"

Pastor Rayburn's approach involved a teaching process. Teaching can be helpful, often enabling clients to see that irrational thoughts cause emotional turmoil. One therapist I know even uses visual aids. He will turn around in his chair, take a rubber snake from his desk drawer, and throw it on the floor near the client. The client may jump or even scream. The counselor then shows the person that the snake is made of rubber. He will explain that how we feel about an object is greatly dependent on how we think about it, that is, whether we identify it as a rubber snake or a real one. I'm not necessarily suggesting this method, but it illustrates well the kind of creativity that a pastor can use in explaining these principles.

It should be noted here that a valuable aid in the learning process is for the pastor to model rational thinking and the process of rational reevaluation. This can be done in all sectors of ministry but especially in the counseling office. Pastor Rayburn, for example, shared with Donald some effective and ineffective ways in which she had handled situations and how her cognitions affected them. She believed wholeheartedly in what she was trying to help Donald achieve in changing his irrational beliefs— otherwise it would not have been effective. It is important to practice what you preach!

Practicing

Eventually the focus of cognitive restructuring needs to shift from educating about the process to actually practicing it. Donald was told that "the proof of the pudding is in the eating," and he would now need to both catch his own irrational thoughts and rethink them. Practice was urged and homework assigned. He accepted specific tasks to guide his practice.

In my counseling I find it helpful to choose instances from the client's own life. I tell clients that when they catch themselves getting upset or depressed, or acting in problematical ways, they should stop at once and find the cue or trigger that set off that behavior. They are to ask themselves: "What irrational idea is at the root of my problem? What unspoken assumption is causing this upset? What am I uncritically telling myself?" This was the thrust of Pastor Rayburn's counseling with Donald:

Pastor: Think back to what you told me about last Friday, when you wanted to ask one of the secretaries at your office for a date after work and you became so upset that you never asked her. You remember that?

Donald: Do I ever! If that keeps happening I'll never ever go out with anyone.

Pastor: OK, try to remember and ask yourself, "What was I telling myself that caused me to be so upset?"

Donald: [Pause] Well, I was embarrassed.

Pastor: Uh-huh. I'll bet you were. But what things were you telling yourself?

Donald: I don't know. [Pause] I don't remember.

Pastor: I know you were saying certain things to yourself, probably not "She hates me, so I can't do it" but

something like that. What do you imagine you were
saying to yourself that stopped you from asking her
and created your anxiety?

Donald: [Pause] I suppose I thought she would say no.
[Pause]

Pastor: Yes! You thought she would say no, and that would
be . . .

Donald: And that would be awful.

Pastor: Would it?

Donald: Yes. . . . Well, no [pause] . . . when you really think
about it. I wouldn't like it, but it wouldn't be *awful.*
[Pause] But it's just that I haven't done anything like
that since I was in high school.

Pastor: I think you're beginning to get the idea. Again, I'd
like you to ask yourself, "What other irrational things
am I telling myself that keep me from approaching
her? How am I hindering myself in asking her out?

As we can see, it generally takes some time at first to help
counselees discover the problematic things they are telling themselves—like Donald's "It would be awful." Notice that Gail
Rayburn responded positively to Donald's groping observations
—she praised his every attempt at identifying an irrational state-
ment. This is very important. If people sense that they are making progress, as the pastor's praise suggests, their situations will
not seem nearly so hopeless. Thus counselees are taught to regard any upset or aberrant behavior as a cue that they may be
operating out of unrealistic beliefs or expectations, and they need
to stop, ferret out the irrational things they have been telling
themselves, and replace them with something rational.

Sometimes it is beneficial if the counselor can play the devil's
advocate. At one point, where Donald seemed quite resistant to
change, Gail Rayburn said, "Let's try something different."
Rising to her feet, she went on: "Let's change chairs. You be the
pastor and I'll be you." Before Donald even had a chance to
consider, much less complain, she was already verbalizing what
she believed to be the irrational things he was thinking, and
suddenly it was Donald's task—acting now as counselor—to
refute them. When I use this technique, I frequently exaggerate

a bit. I formulate the irrational statements as sharply as possible so that clients can see their position as clearly as possible. For some this kind of reversal can often bring great insight.

Counselees do not usually catch cues well at first, and Donald was no exception. Two days after the session, he belatedly had an "aha" experience, suddenly recognizing why he had been upset and what the originating cues actually were. I usually tell clients that they may not catch these cues immediately; I suggest that it may take several days at first, then perhaps several hours, and only after considerable practice will they begin to catch cues right on the spot. Ultimately, though, with enough experience in catching cues and replacing irrational thoughts, the problem is sure to diminish or even disappear.

Additional Cognitive Restructuring Methods

There are several other ways in which the pastor can help counselees change their thinking. I will describe briefly three of them: behavioral rehearsal, imaging, and bibliotherapy.

Behavioral Rehearsal

Behavioral rehearsal (described more fully in chapter 5), or role playing as it is frequently called, has been used to good effect recently in the church by youth groups and education classes and occasionally in pastoral counseling sessions. In behavioral rehearsal the client simply simulates the troublesome situation and runs through the frightening scenario in the counseling session before encountering it in real life.

In the case of Donald Claymore, Pastor Rayburn could have had him practice asking the secretary out for a date. Pastor Rayburn would set up the behavioral rehearsal by first reviewing the scene with Donald, and then suggest that as the scene is being recreated he say out loud the irrational thoughts that occur, then immediately replace them with rational thoughts. The pastor could also tell Donald that she will at times function as his alter ego, his other self, saying out loud some of the things he may be thinking but not verbalizing; and when she does this, he is to incorporate it into his thinking and refute any of the irrational statements. In recreating the situation, Pastor Rayburn could even play the part of the secretary or have Donald play both parts. Where group counseling is involved, another member of the group could become the secretary.

In behavioral rehearsal for cognitive restructuring, the actual words spoken in the back-and-forth conversation are less important than the thinking process of the client, for the aim is to focus and adjust irrational thoughts or beliefs. Such role play provides an effective procedure for presenting new learning experience in a nonthreatening environment.

One important caution, though, about behavioral rehearsal: clients should not take on prematurely situations that are too threatening. If this seems to be a possibility, it is the counselor's responsibility to slow things down by developing a hierarchy or graded list of less stressful situations that can be practiced first, before tackling the troublesome event. In Donald's case, since he already knew the secretary well, an easier or less threatening rehearsal would be just to stop by her desk and say hello. This could be practiced a few times before rehearsing the scenario of asking her out for a date. If even this is too troubling, a still less threatening scene for behavioral rehearsal might be, at home, merely to *think* about saying hello to her the next day.

Imaging

As a counseling technique imaging is often more beneficial than behavioral rehearsal. Imaging is a kind of guided daydream. For example, instead of actually asking the secretary for a date, or even practicing the asking, Donald would simply *imagine* doing it, closing his eyes and visualizing the event as if it were actually occurring. The major difference between daydreaming and imaging, of course, has to do with articulation: in imaging clients are instructed to say out loud all of the events that happen, as well as to express verbally the attendant feelings and the thoughts that occur to them. As with behavioral rehearsal, the pastor acts as a prompter, suggesting thoughts that are perhaps going unverbalized or asking questions which the clients may answer. In imaging, as with behavioral rehearsal or systematic desensitization (described in chapter 5), a hierarchy of increasingly troublesome situations may have to be developed, with successful coping at a lower level followed by progression to the next, more difficult situation. Donald, for example, might image simply smiling at the secretary, before going on to imaging more anxiety-filled scenarios.

When imaging is used in the pastor's office, the clients are first asked to relax and close their eyes. If they appear tense at the beginning, relaxation exercises (described in chapter 2) can be of benefit. Counselees are instructed not to evade a conflict or difficult situation but to "stay with it and see it through."

Next, the counselor verbally portrays the scene, noting a fair amount of detail to help the clients "get into it." If the scene were, for example, Donald asking the secretary to go out, Donald would be instructed to visualize the situation and state in the first person and present tense exactly what is happening. When he begins to feel rising anxiety, or anxiety rises to the point where he desires to flee the situation, this is the moment to stop and take time out for rational restructuring, asking himself, "What irrational ideas am I telling myself that are causing this upset?"

Next, the clients "think aloud" about their situations, describing what is happening and how they feel. Since cognitive restructuring has already taken place, they will generally feel less upset than earlier. If a decrease in upsetness does *not* occur, then the setting may be too threatening (the counselor should start at a lower point on the hierarchy), or the client's identification of the irrational idea was amiss, or the client is not "telling all," or the counselee and counselor have not accurately assessed the troublesome situation and need to do some reevaluation.

Bibliotherapy

A final method for changing cognition is bibliotherapy. I noted earlier, in describing the assessment process, that I ask clients to read books or portions of books to aid in their self-assessment. Donald, like most clients, found a couple of situations in *A New Guide to Rational Living* which were not unlike his own.* Although a number of people find the first half of the book tedious, I urge them to persevere, noting that others have had the same problem but in the end found the book of immeasurable value. Paul Hauck's books—*Overcoming Depression, Overcoming Worry and Fear,* and *Overcoming Frustration and Anger*—are valuable as a second resource, to be read particularly by persons who can identify with the problems addressed.†

In Donald's case, the cognitive restructuring work was quite successful. He was a fairly quick learner and, like many people, once he started having some success in catching his cues and finding emotional relief, there was no turning back. Long-term counseling was not needed. Donald's new way of behaving was self-reinforcing. When he finally got up enough nerve to ask the office secretary out, she turned him down; Donald was nonplussed by her refusal, but, using the principles he had already learned, he handled it so well emotionally that it gave him further confidence to deal with new situations and ultimately to be successful in relating to other women.

Cognitive methods can be quite helpful in counseling. Their effectiveness can be long-lived. And they are particularly appropriate to the counseling done by pastors, whose theological perspective and communal context underscore their interest in and attention to the fundamental matters of thought, attitude, and belief.

4. Helping Parents Help Children

At Ascension Church there was a flurry of interest among the parents of preschool and elementary school children in having a class on "How to Be Good Parents." The Christian education director talked about their wishes with Pastor Dagley. The pastor agreed to teach such a class after convincing another member of the congregation, an elementary school principal, to share in leading the course. In their preparation, the pastor and the principal decided to use *Families,* by Gerald Patterson, a book based on behavior therapy methods.*

Richard Dagley was somewhat apprehensive about teaching behavior therapy concepts, particularly since he had been quite critical of them throughout his brief pastorate. It was not until his coleader, Dr. Sally Hetzel, began to describe how the methods were being used effectively in her school every day that he began to realize that the concepts were "not all that new." Many involved methods he himself had used with his own children— randomly, however, not systematically, and sometimes with quite unintended results.

The best known and most misunderstood of all forms of behavior therapy is an approach to children that is frequently called behavior modification. The term has recently lost favor with many serious therapists because of the way the approach has been abused and because of the tendency to regard and pass off as behavior modification some programs which bear little resemblance to the serious principles upon which they are supposed to be based. As we consider in this chapter parental approaches to children's behavior, we will draw especially upon the reinforcement principles developed by B. F. Skinner and others.† Equally applicable to all ages, these principles are especially effective with children, whose environments are more easily regulated than those of adults.

A Total Approach

It is of first importance in dealing with parent-child problems that the pastor help the parents to recognize and value the infinite worth of the child. Without such an appreciation of transcendent worth, the little person all too frequently becomes nothing more than a "problem," a hindrance to the parents' realization of their own aspirations.

For me, two counseling approaches in addition to behavior therapy have proved especially helpful in this regard. The work of Thomas Gordon in parent effectiveness training is particularly useful for teaching parents to listen to and value what their children say. (In the course offered at their church Dr. Hetzel and Pastor Dagley used sections of Gordon's book that focused on how to listen to your child.*) Equally useful have been the approaches recently developed in the field of conjoint marriage and family counseling.† The emphasis here is upon recognizing the interrelatedness of all the various behaviors within a family: what Father does and says to Mother affects not only the husband-wife relationship but the children as well. For example, the conjoint marriage and family therapist will often see parents who come in with a troubled child, only to discover that in their marriage relationship they have more severe problems than merely the problem with the child. When the marriage as such and the family as a whole begin to function more adequately, many of the "problems" identified with the child seem miraculously to be resolved.

Behavioral methods, when used together with these two more traditional approaches and with a keen sensitivity to children's rights and values, can provide a good total approach to the treatment of children, whether for preventive purposes, as in the course at Ascension Church, or for remedial purposes.

The total approach is integrated to the creation of a calm and reasonable atmosphere in which children and parents alike can begin to feel secure and can understand their freedoms and responsibilities clearly. With a consistent system in which to operate, there is little occasion for parents to explode at their children, piling on verbal and even physical abuse. In such a trust-worthy environment, parents and children are more apt to express affection, communicate differences rationally, and respect each other as individuals.

In teaching behavioral techniques for use with children, I operate on the tacit assumption that parents have certain sets of beliefs, values, and lifestyles that they may ethically pass on to their children. Individuals who disagree with this assumption may have trouble accepting behavioral approaches to children. However, the recent tendency for people to search for their roots suggests that a sense of history and of continuity in cultural and religious values can contribute much to our sense of who we are; without them we feel disoriented and alone. Parents have not only a right but also a responsibility to impart sound values to their children. The use of behavioral techniques can be helpful to that end.

Undertaking to teach these principles to the interested parents of their congregation, Pastor Dagley and Dr. Hetzel spent eight Wednesday evenings with seven sets of parents, most of whom had children in the primary grades. During these sessions the following topics were covered: (1) marriage and the family in the Bible, (2) an understanding of children's growing up processes and what can be expected at different ages, (3) skills of listening and talking to children, (4) the principles of changing and maintaining children's behavior, and (5) specific issues brought up by the parents in the class. Most of the time was spent on topic number four, changing and maintaining behavior, and on how to apply these principles to the specific concerns raised by the parents—bedwetting, messy rooms, temper tantrums, and bedtime woes.

Principles of Behavior Change

Eleven basic principles of behavior change as they apply to children were explained to the parents of Ascension Church, all illustrated by the extensive use of concrete examples (more than can be given here). Pastor Dagley and Dr. Hetzel requested that the class members give examples from their own families by way of further illustration and then ask questions about the behavior problems they were facing with their own children. In the following paragraphs, these principles of behavior change will be presented to the reader much as they were offered to the class. Some of the examples used here were actually brought up by class members in the course of their discussions.*

There are a variety of principles that are useful in strengthening and maintaining desired behavior. The first four concepts mentioned here are especially effective in that regard.

The Positive Reinforcement Principle

A child's behavior will be improved or increased if the occurrence of that behavior is immediately rewarded by a positive consequence. This age-old wisdom is referred to as the positive reinforcement principle.

If your son wipes his wet feet before coming into the house, and you thank him and tell him how much you appreciate it, he has been positively reinforced. Giving him a cookie after he cleans his shoes would also be a positive reinforcement.

Therapists distinguish between primary or extrinsic reinforcers (the cookie) and secondary or intrinsic reinforcers (the "thank you" and your son's own sense of pride). Other primary reinforcers might be food, beverages, candy, and toys—all of which are especially effective with younger children; these extrinsic reinforcers have been used quite successfully in teaching autistic children to talk. Secondary reinforcers such as praise, hugs, gold stars, medals, and trophies have also been found to be quite effective: "That was a good talk," "You did a good job," "I like your shirt"—all foster in children the desire to make an extra effort the next time around (or to wear that shirt again, and soon).

I ask parents, whenever possible, to "catch your children being good" rather than always scolding and punishing them (catch them being bad). Most parents ignore it when their children do what the parents approve, but then immediately get upset when the children act in problematic ways. The best way to increase the incidence of behavior the parents approve is to recognize it instead of ignoring it. This can effectively be done by the use of a primary or secondary reinforcer. If parents learn nothing else but this one principle—to "catch" their children being "good" rather than "bad"—it would be a giant step forward for them in child rearing.

The Negative Reinforcement Principle

A child's behavior will be improved or increased if the occurrence of that behavior is rewarded by the cessation of a negative consequence. This commonsense principle is referred to as negative reinforcement.

A rambunctious son of one of the Ascension parents received negative reinforcement for hanging up his jacket and putting his boots away: he was excused from wiping the dishes that evening. This negative principle functions much like the positive one, except that instead of being reinforced by being given a favorite piece of candy, the child is relieved of a disagreeable chore. The negative reiniforcement serves a positive function in furthering desirable behavior.

The Premack Principle

A behavior highly desired by the parents but hardly desired by the child can be strengthened and increased by making access to one of the child's highly desired activities dependent on performance of the less highly desired behavior. Parents who may never have heard of Premack are doubtless familiar with the principle.

It has been referred to as "Grandmother's law": "You don't get a piece of cake until you eat your peas." "You can go outside and play with Jerry as soon as you have finished cleaning your room." "You can sleep at Mary's house tonight if you get your homework done first."

As I mentioned in the Preface, I am writing this book at a cottage on Lake Vermilion in northern Minnesota. The walleye here bite well in the evening. Evening fishing, for me, is contingent upon my finishing a certain amount of writing each day. When the pace of writing begins to slacken, the possibility of hooking into a four- or five-pound walleye looms and I press on. I do not apply the principle rigidly—there is grace—but it is a form of self-discipline that works well both for children and adults.

Intermittent Reinforcement

When behavior is well established by regular reinforcement, encouragement to continued performance can continue to be given, but with decreased frequency. Intermittent reinforcement means that desired behavior continues to be rewarded, only on a reduced basis.

. When a child is learning a new behavior (like hanging up clothes), continuous reinforcement is best: every time the correct behavior is performed, it is rewarded. Once a behavior is well established, however, switching to an intermittent schedule of reinforcement is beneficial and can actually strengthen the behavior.

Behavior that is continually reinforced may stop quickly if reinforcement should suddenly cease. But if the schedule of reinforcement is gradually stretched, so that more and more performance is required for the same reinforcement and the child cannot predict when reinforcement will occur, then the behavior is likely to be cemented for a long time.

Janet, age seven, was very pleased with the compliments and "special favors" she received each time she cleaned her room. Her parents, members of Ascension Church, were very happy with her performance, but, after a class discussion about intermittent reinforcement, they decided it was time they stopped the continuous rewards, especially the special favors she was receiving. They did this by stretching the reinforcement schedule, giving her at first continued words of praise but fewer special favors. Then, after a while, when Janet no longer expected special favors for cleaning her room, they began also to praise her less frequently. It is important to note that there was still positive reinforcement for the cleaning she did, but it came less frequently and at unexpected intervals. For the child, intermittent reinforcement works something like a slot machine: you never know whether the next time you make the right motions you will hit the jackpot.

Besides these four principles used effectively for strengthening and maintaining desired behavior, there are principles that are effective in weakening or stopping unwanted behavior. We will mention four of them as well.

The Principle of Punishment

A child's behavior can be weakened if it is immediately followed by a negative consequence or the removal of a positive consequence. Most parents need little incentive to pursuing this principle of punishment.

Parents have spanked their kids, berated them, nagged them, yelled at them, scolded them, hit them, and ridiculed them. In short, punishment has perhaps been the primary way in which parents have sought to mold the character of the younger generation. It has worked at times, but it has also backfired. The advantage of spanking Tim and telling him not to hit his brother is that, for a short time at least, Tim stops hitting his brother. The disadvantage is that the behavior is not permanently stopped by this approach, and Tim will have to be yelled at and spanked again because he will hit his brother again.

When a child has learned a desired behavior and is able to do it well, but hasn't actually stopped the inappropriate behavior, punishment can be used effectively. But punishment often encourages the development of escape behavior or avoidance behavior that can be worse than the original problem. It can cause the child to have "bad me" feelings or even greater psychological problems. Frequently the punished child just finds an alternative and sometimes more aggressive activity with which to resist the parent. Punishment frequently tends to separate child and parent rather than bringing them together.

Should you never punish? Not necessarily. For centuries punishment was the primary mode of control in child rearing. Conversely, in the Freud-Spock era of "permissive child rearing," children often did what they wanted, there being little parental interference. With no new method of control to substitute for punishment, the permissive approach proved unsatisfactory. Lacking guidance or discipline from their parents, some children floundered, acting in ways that were not only upsetting to their families and to society but also hurtful to themselves. The methods described in this chapter offer a more constructive alternative.

There are some forms of punishment which, if used sparingly and thoughtfully, can be beneficial in child rearing. One of the most helpful, called "time out," has recently been refined by behavior therapists. It is similar in some ways to the older approach of "Go to your room and stay there until you have a better attitude." Time out, however, is explained to a child beforehand and is applied only for those offenses that have been specifically detailed. It usually involves taking the child out of his or her normal environment for a short period of time—perhaps five minutes—to a dull room where it is not possible either to find amusement or to continue the problem behavior. The purpose is to remove any possibility of reinforcing the undesirable activity. Any such punishment should of course be part of a concurrent positive reinforcement program.

The Principle of Satiation

If a child is allowed (or required) to perform a behavior until tiring of it, the behavior will become weakened. The principle may be new to some parents.

Little did I know, as a 100-pound nine-year-old, what I was in for when I set fire to the vacant lot next door. By design, I was also the hero who found and reported the fire, and I did not expect to be caught so easily. Neither could I have anticipated my mother's way of handling it. Producing three big boxes of farmer's matches and a three-pound coffee can, she told me: "I want you to light every single match, blow it out, and put it in this can." Fantastic, I thought. But by the time I had emptied one box the fun was gone and I yearned to be with my friends. I told Mom that I had lit enough matches, but she firmly insisted that I light all of them. It took a *long* time. Ever since, I not only have no urge to set things on fire; I don't even get a thrill out of stirring sticks in a campfire. My wife (who jokingly calls herself a dedicated pyromaniac) thinks I can't light a proper blaze in the fireplace.

My mother was not familiar with "the principle of satiation," but she was surely practicing it in a way that effectively reduced an undesirable behavior. Not all undesirable behaviors are stopped that simply, but the principle of satiation can be a useful method for weakening an unwanted activity.

The Principle of Extinction

To lessen or stop a certain behavior, arrange the child's environment so that he or she will receive no reinforcement for that behavior. This could require considerable effort on the part of the parent.

As parents, we often do things backwards. When the three-year-old is playing quietly with the five-year-old, we breathe a sigh of relief and scurry to get some work done, or just collapse for a few minutes of rest, but then we yell at the children when they start fighting again. This means that when they are peaceful, we ignore them, but when they are doing something we don't like, we give them our undivided attention. A diametrically opposite approach is to be preferred. It would be better to praise the children for their quiet play and, unless they are hurting each other seriously, ignore their scraps.

Jim and Fran Robinson asked the Ascension class about how to help their two-year-old son stop his temper tantrums. It was suggested by Dr. Hetzel that they simply ignore the tantrums and, when possible, leave the room—and that this be done in public as well. (Also suggested were positive ways in which the Robinsons could give their son attention.) Fran and Jim agreed to try it, and within two weeks reported almost complete cessation of the tantrums. It was a struggle for the parents, but they knew they had to be consistent and never give in to the child's ploys for attention. Fran related that when he wanted something in a grocery store and threw one of his tantrums, she just walked into the next aisle. At first, he would pick himself up, go to where she was, and resume his tantrum; but soon he came to realize that even that was of no use—he would be ignored unless he came and talked to his parents calmly.

Altering the environment may create a bigger task for the parents than for the child, but it can produce results. It can extinguish, not the child, but the behavior that is sometimes so intolerable.

The Principle of Incompatible Behavior

A child's problematic behavior can be weakened if an incompatible behavior is rewarded. Parents have used this concept for centuries.

The point is to set up an either/or for the child, whether in terms of time or of substance. Parents have often tickled their children or clowned in order to make crying children laugh. A behavioral therapist will advise parents that rather than scolding or spanking a child caught playing with an electrical outlet, they should simply invite the youngster's attention to something more interesting.

Elaine Wilkins, one of the parents in the Ascension class, had a three-year-old girl who loved to sing. Amy also loved to get in trouble just when her mother was in the middle of some demanding household task. Dr. Hetzel suggested that at such times Elaine might initiate a sing-along which would interest and involve Amy and be incompatible with her nuisance behavior. After one week Elaine reported that she herself was getting tired of singing the same songs over and over, but that while the singing was going on, Amy was so peacefully preoccupied with the song that she stayed out of her mother's hair.

Parents need not be defeated by behavior which is incompatible with their values or sense of well-being. They can seek to displace it by other behavior which is incompatible from the standpoint of the child's own interests or time frame.

Certain principles are used not so much for encouraging or discouraging existent behavior as for developing new behaviors. Three such principles are particularly worth mentioning.

The Cuing Principle

A new behavior will be learned when a cue is received immediately prior to the occurrence of the hoped-for behavior. Parents have long been "cuing" their children in regard to "manners."

When our daughter was three and we were trying to teach her to be polite at the table, we prompted her to say "please" before we passed her something, and "thank you" after she had received it. Once she knew the words, we could just ask, "What do you say?" and she would obediently say her pleases and thank yous, but with little energy or meaning. Then, one afternoon when we were out for a drive, we bought three ice cream cones instead of the usual two. For the first time, there was a whole cone for Chrissy. When she realized that instead of sharing ours, she would be having a cone of her own, she turned to me and exclaimed with real enthusiasm: "*Thank* you, Daddy!" She said it with such joy and meaning that it brought tears to my eyes. Chrissy had learned the meaning of *thanks*. Of course, on occasion she continued to need further cuing.

Cuing can be used for a variety of behaviors. It can involve either verbal cues ("say thank you") or physical cues (a firm hand on the shoulder in church to remind a child just learning to be quiet during the worship service). After a cue is given and the desired behavior follows, it is important that the parent reward the child with praise, a hug, or some other positive reinforcer.

The Principle of Shaping

Rewarding successive approximations of a desired behavior will assist a child in learning the new behavior. Like the rest of us, children too need encouragement to keep trying—and a sense of success along the way.

One of the families in Pastor Dagley's class had a boy, six-year-old Michael, who was physically not as well coordinated as some children. Michael's father was a high school letterman from a small town in Iowa, and Gordon was determined to make his boy into an athlete. When they played baseball in the back yard, Gordon would throw the ball faster than Michael could handle it. The boy would get frightened and want to quit playing. This would anger Gordon, who would call Michael a sissy and throw even harder, until his son fell or was hit by the ball and went crying to his mother. Mom would get angry at Dad. Everyone would be upset—and the boy was learning not to play ball but to fear it.

Class members criticized Gordon for his insistence that the boy "be a man" in such a narrowly defined sense. They thought Gordon should be more willing to allow Michael to be himself; the child should not be expected to be a carbon copy of his father. Gordon seemed willing to reconsider his attitudes. In the meantime Sally Hetzel explained a way of teaching children to play ball (in itself a worthwhile goal) by successive approximation—which could at least reduce the tension in their home. She suggested first rolling the ball, rolling it gently until Michael learned to catch it well and then rolling it more firmly. Next, the father was to toss the ball underhand very gently and reinforce his son every time Michael came even close to catching it—not just when he actually caught it. Gordon was only very gradually to increase the speed of the toss (throw) and the difficulty of receiving it, until Michael actually learned to catch.

The same process was to be repeated with batting. In this way the boy could learn at his own pace, without fear, rather than at the pace his father (a natural athlete) remembered having learned. What is more, Michael would develop enough skill so that he could later make his own choice about whether or not to participate in athletics. He could decide not from a position of failure and fear but from a position of competence and freedom.

The Modeling Principle

A new behavior will be learned when the child observes a prestigeful person performing the desired behavior. The importance of models for learning has long been recognized in most areas of life.

To further help Gordon in teaching his son to play ball, Dr. Hetzel suggested that if Michael had a baseball hero it would further motivate him in his learning process. She recommended that Gordon invite the boy to attend a professional baseball game. If he went and enjoyed it, with repeated similar outings he might develop heroes from among the local superstars. Frequently having a hero leads a child to attempt the behavior of the hero: taking jumps off the front porch like a favorite motorcyclist or skier, or eating the breakfast cereal of a decathlon champion, or even—what I tried as a kid—chewing tobacco like a big-league pitcher. Our Chris is now a great admirer of long-distance swimmers, particularly women, and this summer when an English Channel swimmer was much in the news she swam to an island far out in the lake—something she probably would never have accomplished at our urging!

Modeling is a principle worth remembering for parents. Like cuing and shaping, it can be especially helpful in relation to the learning of new behaviors.

The Counseling Process

The principles of behavior change which were explained and introduced in the parent education class at Ascension can also serve as a basis for the pastor's counseling of families. Pastors will usually find parents receptive to the concepts and eager to work at them. Use of the behavioral methods in relation to children will of course alter somewhat the pattern of traditional counseling procedures.

In some early forms of child counseling, the therapist would see the child only, without the parent being present. Later it was realized that parents should frequently be involved. This sometimes led to the formation of parent groups, and therapists would actually offer counsel to the parents.

Therapy for children next advanced tremendously with the appearance of an approach to counseling which dealt with entire family units rather than isolated individuals. The approach quickly proved its usefulness as therapists discovered the importance of working with the whole family at one time in the therapy process—a "systems approach" that ministers have known for generations. Viewing the interaction of all family members is not only beneficial for helping the counselor assess the problem, but frequently the entire family's style of interaction has to be altered if the child's behavior is to be changed.

Behavior therapy now goes one step further. Although seeing the whole family initially for assessment, the behavior therapist subsequently deals mainly with the parents as those leaders of the family who hold the key to any change in the children. The parents are taught systematically to apply the above-mentioned eleven principles of behavioral change to the specific problem or problems they are encountering with their children. Since the child's environment is actively, if unwittingly, reinforcing certain behaviors at all times, neither the child nor the therapist is in the best position to bring about change. And parents are the most important single factor in that environment. In effect, therefore, the behavioral counselor of children serves as an educator, a consultant to the parents (and teachers if necessary), assisting them in regaining control of the family environment and helping the child to resolve his or her behavior problems.

The actual process of behavioral counseling in relation to children's problems begins, as in the case of adults, with a period of assessment. The specific problem behavior needs to be defined and its frequency of occurrence noted. Establishing the frequency helps parents and counselor get a realistic understanding of the extent of the problem. It also offers a base line against which to measure the effectiveness of any treatment. This is important in order to determine whether a specific counseling approach is working or whether other methods need to be initiated.

The assessment process means, first, defining the problem behavior in terms of its excesses (for undesirable activities) or deficiencies (for hoped-for behaviors), and then counting the number of times each particular problem occurs in a given period and recording that data on a chart. This measuring should be done over a period of three or four days at a minimum, both when establishing a base line and later during the treatment process. It needs to be done at the same time each day, and for a specific length of time, since the occurrence of the problem behavior may vary according to the child's or the family's schedule.

For example, Greg beats up on his sister. That's a problem behavior. His mother notes each day on a chart the number of times Greg picks a fight with Alice from the moment he gets home from school until they all sit down to dinner. This two-to-three-hour chart is kept for five consecutive days. In the case of a problem behavior that occurs much more frequently than Greg's, a chart based on only an hour a day may suffice. If the problem behavior occurs infrequently, the time frame for measurement may have to be a full day.

I suggest to some parents that rather than putting check marks on a tablet, they simply use a golf counter to keep track. It is also good for both husband and wife to take turns counting the incidents, so that both parents are involved in the process. It is often helpful if, at the same time, they chart their own related behaviors—such as how many positive reinforcers they offer the child. This helps to broaden the focus so that it is not limited to the child's problem alone but also includes the fact that the parents are reinforcing undesirable behaviors or are not cuing and reinforcing the desired ones.

After the assessment process is well advanced, parents are taught the principles of behavior change for children. Persuasiveness may be required on the part of the pastor to help them see that *they* (not the minister) are the change agents and that improvement in the child's behavior will be dependent upon them. Often parents want to dump the problem child at the door of the church or counseling agency, figuring that, as one of the last institutions interested in what is good and right, it will be eager to do and will indeed have to do what they themselves have been unable to do—make their child behave. Parents learning the principles of behavior change in relation to children need education and motivation to see change as a possibility for themselves.

If the parents agree to the change process, the next step is for them to refine their definition of the child's problem behavior, being more specific than before in their description and perhaps altering their definition as they observe the behavior more carefully, and then develop a plan of change, systematically introducing the new behaviors to the child and practicing them with the child. It is the pastor's task to help the parents choose humane goals for the child by pointing out instances in which they are unwittingly passing on to the child the "sins" of their own childhoods. It is also the pastor's task, as consultant, to coach the parents in their change work, helping them to hone their change-producing skills and encouraging them to persevere. Parents frequently don't do well at first, but there is nothing like even a little success to increase their motivation and confidence. Behavioral rehearsal (see chapter 5) can be used with the mother and father by having them practice their interaction with the child in your office before they return home and use the principles there.

Once change has begun to occur, both child and parents are encouraged by their success. Parents are urged to make other changes in the parent-child relationship, changes that are based not on catching the child being "bad" but on rewarding the constructive behaviors and doing together things that are emotionally nourishing for all. With the advent of change in a child's behavior, I often ask parents if they want to apply the principles they have just learned to some problem of their own. For example, if the parents are overweight, they may wish to use such behavior therapy methods to change their own eating habits. The child, observing the parents working responsibly towards a solution of their grown-up behavior problems, will be further encouraged in the learning of new and more constructive actions. The principles of behavior change are not just for children. They can work for everyone.

5. Other Behavioral Methods

There is always the danger in any book on counseling of attempting too much. So much material may be covered that nothing will be useful to the reader. Since the purpose of this book, however, is simply to whet your appetite for behavioral methods in pastoral counseling and invite you to read further in the literature of behavior therapy, I would like to explore briefly several additional methods which are potentially beneficial to the pastor's counseling ministry.

Systematic Desensitization

A psychology professor I know once told his class that if they could say "systematic desensitization" ten times fast, he would give them an *A* for the course. He knew that the high-sounding term and the seeming difficulty of using the method—designed mainly for dealing with people's fears—has actually frightened many people away. In truth, if the procedure is broken down into small components and used with general therapeutic sensitivity, it is not too difficult to master. The components include: (1) relaxation (sometimes omitted), (2) explanation of the method to the counselee, (3) developing a "hierarchy" of troubling events, and (4) imaging. To illustrate these components as they function in a therapeutic situation, let me share with you a case which was treated by a pastoral counseling specialist. Although the case itself may seem unusual, it provides a good illustration of how systematic desensitization works.

A California minister referred a forty-six-year-old real estate saleswoman, Maggie Coleman, to the pastoral counseling center. She had been visiting a psychotherapist for six months, and a hypnotist before that, without results. She was married but saw little of her husband, a computer programming consultant who traveled extensively. Her problem was fear. Maggie had a great fear that in public situations she would have an intense urge to urinate and would find it awkward or difficult or impossible to excuse herself for doing so. She did in fact urinate frequently, two to three times an hour as a matter of routine precaution, so that if someone came into her presence, she wouldn't be embarrassed by having to excuse herself to go to the bathroom. She made a point of never leaving home or office for more than half an hour at a time—an awkward problem for someone whose job was to sell real estate. Maggie always made certain that she urinated before going out with a prospective customer or before the appointed hour for someone to visit her in her office. If the people she was expecting were late, she would urinate every ten minutes until they arrived. Always, the first thing she did when she reached a destination or place was to scout out the restroom. She almost stopped going to church, movies, and concerts and flying in airplanes, because of her fear. She felt as if every eye in the place were looking at her every time she headed for the toilet and that people "made untoward comments about me." Maggie sometimes urinated as many as fifty times a day.

Careful assessment disclosed no major traumatic event that could be identified as the cause of the phobia. It had developed gradually over the last two to three years. Maggie's previous counseling also had found no trauma, only a possible relationship between her husband's travels and the onset of her difficulties.

Classic systematic desensitization seemed to be indicated. It can often be beneficial in the case of such fears and phobias, situations where anxiety is conditioned, yet there is no actual danger: fear of flying, close places (claustrophobia), examinations, crowds, being watched by others, talking before large groups of people. Maggie Coleman was willing to try it.

She was first trained in relaxation by a biofeedback therapist while the history of her problems and a hierarchy of anxiety-producing events was being developed by other members of the staff. It was during her relaxation training, and after the assessment of her problem, that the decision to use systematic desensitization was made and its process explained. Maggie was told that the basis for desensitization is the fact that an image can functionally represent the real-life situation. Therefore, when she learned to "image" being in a public place for several hours without any concern or anxiety about urinating, she would be able to duplicate the experience in real life, also without any anxiety.

From her pastoral counselor's notes about her history and from Maggie's own listing of possible items, they developed together a list of troublesome events. Her husband too was asked to help. Between sessions he was to look at her list of anxiety-provoking situations and add to it. At the next session the lengthy list was pruned to seventeen items. The counselor then asked Maggie to rank these seventeen in order, beginning with those that caused the greatest amount of anxiety and ending with those that occasioned the least anxiety. The result was Maggie's hierarchy of troubling events and situations:

1. A long plane trip that is so bumpy that the Fasten Seat Belts sign is on continually and she has a powerful urge to urinate.
2. A long car trip where she has to request others to stop the car so she can urinate.
3. A slightly shorter car trip with her husband and another couple where she does not actually request stopping but is worried that she might have to.
4. A concert where she is in the center of a long row of seats, far from the aisle.
5. The center of the row in a darkened movie theater.
6. In the middle of a lecture at a local college.
7. Dinnertime on an airplane when the stewardesses are serving refreshments and their carts fill the aisle.
8. At church in the middle of the sermon when she has difficulty concentrating and feels she has to go to the bathroom.
9. Taking tennis lessons in the evening, where in the midst of a two-hour session with her husband she feels she has to urinate.
10. Watching her husband play an evening basketball game at the gym.
11. In the fitting room trying on some clothes while shopping for a new dress.

12. During on-the-job errands in the car, for example, to drop something off at the printers or at the post office.
13. Visiting her mother-in-law's home.
14. Eating at a restaurant with her husband.
15. Visiting her mother's house on a Sunday afternoon.
16. At home with her husband, watching TV.
17. Eating a bowl of ice cream in the kitchen when no one else is home.

After Maggie Coleman had learned to relax, understood the concept of systematic desensitization, and developed a hierarchy, the actual desensitization procedure began. At the beginning of a counseling session, she was asked to practice relaxation exercises for five to ten minutes. While she was relaxing, with her eyes closed, item number seventeen at the bottom of the list was presented. The counselor did not simply mention the item but actually described the scene, using as many details as possible to help make it come alive. Maggie was also urged to add any further details to make the situation as vivid as possible; she was to visualize the room where the scene takes place, the arrangements of the furniture, even attendant tastes or smells if they could help her recapitulate the experience and feel as if she were really there.

Some individuals have difficulty visualizing a scene or event at first, and a few never develop the skill. I suggest to people that they think of imaging as having a daydream while listening to a boring speech: for a few moments you are transported to another place and time, reliving the past or fantasizing the future. Maggie practiced imaging the bottom-ranked item first and then gradually moved to other items just above it. Practicing gives people a chance to develop the skill in connection with events which are likely to cause comparatively little anxiety.

After the image has been described and imaged, it is necessary to assess and identify the attendant feelings. The counselor says, "If the imaging triggers even the slightest anxiety or fear, raise your left index finger. If none, do nothing."

Maggie Coleman had little trouble learning to image. Each scene was presented for only fifteen to thirty seconds, even less if it appeared she was becoming uncomfortable. After each presentation she was told, "OK, now banish the scene from your mind and just relax. Feel yourself very calm and relaxed." After a fifteen- to forty-five-second pause the scene was presented again. After the situation could be imaged for two to four times without any feeling of disturbance, the next higher item in the hierarchy was introduced.

Maggie had little trouble with the bottom four items on her list. Most of the counseling time—four sessions—was spent on the next five situations. Patiently they were presented over and over again, with constant encouragement from the counselor, until Maggie began to feel comfortable also with them. By the time she arrived at the final eight items, they moved fairly quickly and, because of her practiced skill in imaging, triggered little anxiety. Finally, when the top-ranked item, a long-distance flight, could be presented to her without anxiety, a final procedure known as "flooding" was used. Together Maggie and her pastoral counselor created the most "god-awful possible" scene they could conjure, and she was asked to visualize it— realizing that she would have some anxiety but knowing that she could handle it. The scene she chose was flying on a ten-hour transatlantic flight which was so rough that the passengers could not leave their seats for any reason. She experienced some anxiety but was not troubled by it, having learned through much practice that she could actually live with a measure of anxiety and not panic. Systematic desensitization had enabled her to visualize all the items in her hierarchy without appreciable distress.

Besides the procedures of imaging used in the office, Maggie was urged gradually to expose herself to real-life situations where she would be likely to encounter her concern about urinating, for example, going to a movie and sitting in the center of a row, or going to a meeting and not immediately seeking out a rest-room. Each week the counselor asked her, "What challenge will you take on this week?" If she did not ask enough of herself, he would urge her—but never force her—to do more. If she took on too much, he would trim her task to a more realistic level.

Finally, after ten weeks of counseling, a fortuitous event occurred. A relative died in a distant city. Maggie was required to make a two-hour plane trip to attend the funeral. As luck would have it, the flight was rough and the Fasten Seat Belts sign was on almost all the time. Immediately Maggie experienced the old anxiety. At first she thought that all her counseling had been for nothing and that she hadn't learned anything. But then in a flash she realized that it was not the situation that was intolerable, it was she who was upsetting herself! Suddenly she knew she could handle the situation . . . and she did! After three more weeks of counseling, Maggie was urinating normally. Her fears of being out in crowds disappeared, and she felt like a new person. She who had once resigned herself to unending anxiety about urination now exclaimed, "I've been given a new life."

Variations of Systematic Desensitization

A variation of systematic desensitization using "self-control" was developed by Goldfried in 1971.* In traditional imaging, a scene is presented in its entirety for the client, with a view to reducing the person's anxiety about the situation. In the self-control variation, a setting with inherent anxiety is introduced, but the client is urged, even while imaging, to resolve the situation and bring it to completion. In taking responsibility for the solution as well as for the conquering of anxiety, the person is less dependent upon the counselor. The client is being taught to cope, in the words of Goldfried, "with anxiety responses and cues rather than with situations which elicit the tension."† For example, Donald Claymore (whom we met in chapter 3) could have been presented with the imaginary scene of standing by the secretary's desk and wanting to ask her out. He would then be asked to finish the story, telling what comes next and bringing the situation to a resolution—and in so doing reducing his anxiety.

Another variation of systematic desensitization might involve the use of graded steps in actual situations. The parish pastor who does not wish to use classic systematic desensitization may find it beneficial simply to expose phobic individuals gradually to the actual feared or anxiety-producing events. We all know someone who was afraid of water but learned to swim by being thrown into a pool. Unfortunately, most people who are afraid of water would by that device either drown or find their fear intensified. But individuals who are exposed to a feared situation only gradually, and are trained to relax at the same time, can unlearn their fear.

A foreign student in an eastern college had developed tremendous shyness with women. In his own country, Max had little difficulty relating to the opposite sex, but after a few feeble and abortive attempts to date American students, he acquired a strong fear of even looking at a woman. The campus pastor devised a treatment plan whereby Max was placed in a mixed-sex counseling group and then assigned specific tasks sequenced in graded steps. They constituted a hierarchy of systematic desensitization, ranging from the most scary to the easiest:

1. Ask a woman for a date.
2. Walk up to a mixed group of unknown students and begin a conversation with one of the women.
3. Sit across from a woman at lunch. Say hi and smile, then add two or three comments about the food, followed by a few questions about some course she is taking (their substance to be gleaned from noticing the books at her side).
4. Sit across from a woman student at lunch. Say hi and smile; then make two or three comments about the food.
5. Sit across from a woman student at lunch. Say hi and smile.
6. Sit across from a woman student at lunch, without necessarily talking to her or even looking at her.

Each task, beginning with number six, was done two to four times successfully before moving on to the next level. Level two proved too difficult a step; Max balked at it and did not practice his assignment. Further practice at step three, with the addition of a few more comments about the food and classes, proved to be necessary before he was able to start moving up the hierarchy again.

Before Max began to talk even briefly with a woman student—at each step in his systematic desensitization schedule—the approach was first practiced in the office. At the beginning the counselor took the part of a woman student, and Max only had to sit in the same room, saying nothing. The initial anxiety resulting from doing even this much was almost too high, but manageable. In time they gradually moved up his hierarchy until in role play Max was himself asking a woman for a date, at first clumsily but later with some adeptness. If his counselor had started him at the top of the hierarchy, the attempt would have backfired and the counseling would have been counterproductive. As it turned out, the graded-step approach to role playing and reality testing allowed the systematic desensitization to occur to Max's complete satisfaction and delight.

Behavioral Rehearsal

One of the most unsound assumptions on the part of change agents, be they pastors preaching, educators teaching, or therapists counseling, is that if a person gains a new understanding of something, receives a fresh insight, he or she will automatically change. But frequently this is not the case. People do not automatically change after learning of their need to change, and often the reason they do not is their uncertainty and anxiety about how to get started and how to go about it. It is possible to teach yourself to play golf, but it is immensely helpful to have an experienced player with you the first few times you try it. Otherwise, when you swing the club, you might easily become discouraged about excavating the turf instead of driving the ball 280 yards in a straight line. What is needed is a transition between knowing and doing.

In behavior therapy behavioral rehearsal supplies this need. Otherwise known as role playing, this approach to simulating interpersonal situations goes back as far as the early 1800s.*

I personally began employing behavioral rehearsal during my training as a counselor. A supervisor remarked that my counseling was sound but had the finesse of a bull in a china shop: whenever I felt behavioral rehearsal could be beneficial in the counseling process, I would abruptly say, "I think we need to do some role playing," and almost without explanation I would dive right into it. What I found, after blitzing ahead, was that my client was left back on the diving board, trembling, unwilling to leap in. I would then do a quick retreat and try to coerce, cajole, plead, or beg. But by that time resistance had already built up, fears had developed, and there was no way that the person would participate.

The use of behavioral rehearsal requires considerable finesse. To begin with, it cannot be used until the client is convinced that the new behavior is a good thing to learn. That's important! To jump from assessment of a junior executive's problem to behavioral rehearsal involving assertiveness with her boss will doom the learning process to failure unless that junior executive learns the potential benefit of being assertive with her boss.

Once clients are convinced of the value of the desired behavior, I gently explain the technique of behavioral rehearsal. As much as possible I allow it to come up naturally in the conversation we are having about the desired changes. I describe it as a dry run, much like practicing a speech in front of a mirror or trying a golf swing without a ball. I also relate how it has been helpful with previous clients, citing someone who had difficulty "getting into" behavioral rehearsal at first but eventually found it helpful. Telling the clients that in behavioral rehearsal I *expect* them to be awkward at first, and not say all the right things, I add: "But it's better that we do it here first, where it doesn't count, than out there where it does."

The resistance to using behavioral rehearsal can be great, so preparations are necessary unless a client has previously used the procedure with a measure of success. Some people refuse to believe that practicing in the office can really help. When someone tells me "It's artificial," I agree: "Yes, it *is* artificial, but what you are learning and the feelings that result are real." One time, as I was training a group of counselors, a male and female trainee—who had not known each other previously—developed such strong feeling towards each other in doing behavioral rehearsal (they were role playing a husband and wife with marital problems) that they actually had to stay after class for "debriefing."

Frequently the new behavior is easily defined and requires little preparation beyond actually practicing it. A father can redo a parent-child fight in which he kicked his daughter out of the house. He would start over again and try a different way of handling the disagreement, perhaps several different ways leading to quite different results. In the case of Max, the foreign student described above who had developed tremendous anxiety about meeting women, a hierarchy of practice scenes had to be developed.

Pastors who have worked with small children in parish education programs may already be familiar with role playing. But let me make a few suggestions for using behavioral rehearsal in the counseling process:

1. Try to pick scenes in which the clients are the initiators of action rather than being acted upon, for example, where they strike up a conversation with someone they fear rather than having the feared person approach them.
2. As noted before, if the desired behavior is complex or very troublesome, develop a hierarchy of scenes and begin at the bottom, moving up at a gradual pace which will stretch the clients without making them uncomfortable.
3. It is frequently beneficial for individuals new to behavioral rehearsal to try "warm up" scenes which pose no threat, so that acquaintance with the technique will calm the stage fright and uncertainties they may otherwise feel.
4. As noted with imaging and systematic desensitization, use as many details as necessary to make the scenes vivid. Instruct people who are redoing a troublesome event of the past to use the same situational background in a fresh way, not replaying the scene but approaching it as if it never happened before.
5. Urge your clients to stay within the scene even if they become fearful or want to flee. Have them express their fears and then rethink the situation in fresh scenarios until they are not so intimidated.
6. It is best for you, the counselor, not to play a part in a scene but to have someone else do it, so that you can coach the clients while they are acting out their roles. Unfortunately, unless the client is in a group session or has family members along, the task is generally up to you. If you *are* in the scene, move to another chair as a way of symbolically saying that you are for the moment taking a new part. When I finish playing the part of a particularly disagreeable character, I usually move back to my former chair with the comment: "Whew! I'm glad I don't have to play him (or her) anymore!"
7. Sometimes it is helpful to model or demonstrate the desired behavior, assuming this can be done. I will occasionally attempt to model for one spouse alternative ways of

treating the other. Sometimes people don't make changes for the simple reason that they just don't know where to begin. In modeling a new approach or style, you give them the "nuts and bolts" of how to act differently.

8. Sometimes anxious individuals need to practice relaxation, either beforehand or right in the middle of a scene. Use some of the methods described earlier to help them relax before proceeding with the rehearsal.

9. Role reversal, when husband plays wife and vice versa, or mother plays daughter and vice versa, can be a real eye-opener. Although this does not give clients practice in a new behavior, it does help each to see what the other feels and how difficult it is to be that person.

After a scene has been practiced, two things remain: First, the client and counselor talk about how well it was played, and suggestions are elicited for improving the behavior. Second, the client is urged to go and act the same way in the outside world; this becomes a homework assignment for the coming week.

It is useful to do first in the counselor's office what has been and may still be a frightening thing outside. Behavioral rehearsal is especially suited to situations like practicing new assertive behavior, applying for a job, giving speeches, and meeting people in public. It is helpful in family relationships for practicing different ways of relating. It is beneficial to individuals who feel inept in socializing, who in the process of maturation have not picked up the commonly accepted attitudes, mores, and interpersonal skills which allow one to function effectively among other people. It can help those who lack the skill to do some of the things most people take for granted. For example, I use it with shy or withdrawn adolescents to help them in their heterosexual relationships. It can be as simple as saying hi or asking a friend to dance. What is more, people are better inclined to practice the concepts we talk about in the session if there has been behavioral rehearsal first.

Problem Solving

Joe and Linda Hernandez cared for each other but had been having difficulty communicating with one another for the past four or five years. They recognized the problem and were open to opportunities for addressing it. They had even attended a marriage enrichment seminar sponsored by their church. Held at a rustic retreat center, complete with fireplace, nestled in the pines on the banks of a babbling brook, it was truly a mountain-top experience. Here they learned specific skills in communication which helped them greatly to speak clearly to one another and to understand each other, thus relieving what they thought had been a key problem in their marriage.

After they came down from the mountain, however, Linda and Joe made an unsettling discovery: Having become better communicators and having clearly told each other what they wanted to see changed, they could bring no resolution to their differences. The problems were still there. All they could do now was communicate better about them!

Knowing the problem but being unable to solve it is a common difficulty, especially for reasonably sensitive, insightful people. Education in methods of problem solving can usually help such people. Joe and Linda were fortunate that their parish priest was both knowledgeable and experienced in this regard—able to teach them enough about problem solving so they could begin to help themselves find compromises and solutions for their differences. Through educational counseling in problem-solving skills, a basically sound marriage was prevented from bogging down in frustration. Like relaxation and communication, the ability to solve and resolve problems is a useful skill for effective living.

There are certain groups of people who have of necessity developed especially good skills in problem solving. Attorneys and business people, for example, frequently make more effective crisis counselors than other individuals because they are able to solve problems rapidly and in a reasonable and rational manner. Many people—including some counselors and ministers—do not have a systematic skill in this area. For them particularly I would outline the following five-step method of problem solving—there are others, of course—which I have found effective in my own counseling:*

Goals

The first step in problem solving is to establish a goal or goals. This changes the counseling approach from negative (problems to be done away) to positive (goals to be achieved). Individuals can develop specific and measurable objectives toward which the problem-solving efforts will be aimed. Short-term, easily attained goals are more helpful than unrealistic, long-term goals, which often invite failure.

Resources

The next step is to take inventory of the internal and external resources available in working toward these goals. Internal resources include inner strengths and skills, coping methods, and successful past experiences with problem solving. All of us have gone through numerous problem situations in our lives, many of them successfully. We can speak personally of what we know at firsthand and thereby help other individuals dig for the memory of their own past experiences.

External resources are found in people's environments: church, community groups and agencies, family and friends, school, money. These various persons, groups, and resources offer much in the way of advice, assistance, moral support, and gratification as people seek to work through difficult situations. The inventory should include how these resources can be used—whether for technical assistance, an understanding ear, or fun and companionship.

Alternatives

Once the goals have been established and a person's resources cataloged, it is time to broaden awareness of the many possibilities available for resolving the problem situation. In a brainstorming session, the person is encouraged to come up with as many ideas as possible. All the alternatives, whether feasible or not, are listed. Sometimes a client's thinking may be so clouded by distress that the minister needs to suggest some possible courses of action just to jar the person into seeing how many choices are open.

After the various alternative courses of action have been listed and brainstormed, the list is narrowed. It is first reduced by crossing out any possibilities that go against the person's ethics or value system. For example, if the problem is that a family does not have enough money to live on, but husband and wife cherish the time they have together, then moonlighting by either of them would be incompatible with their values and would have to be ruled out as a potential solution.

The potential effectiveness of the listed alternatives is also weighed. With additional information provided out of the minister's own fund of experience, individuals can evaluate the degree to which each of the available alternatives might aid them in actually reaching their desired goals. It is important not to dismiss any alternative too quickly, since there are instances in which a combination of two possible courses of action may be just what the situation requires. Pastor and parishioner together narrow the list to those altenatives that are most likely to be effective.

Commitment to Action

After cataloging and evaluating various alternatives, it is important that the client choose among them and then make a commitment to embark upon one or two specific courses of action. This commitment needs to be quite firm, even documented in the form of a written contract. If necessary a particular course of action may be further broken down into small, concrete steps to be taken toward solving the problem. This too should be spelled out in the commitment.

Once a definite commitment has been made, the individual must take action. Counselees need to overcome passivity and get beyond any dependence on the counselor. Acting towards a solution, whether they feel like it or not, is essential to that end. To quote Hobart Mowrer, "It is easier to act your way into a new way of feeling than to feel your way into a new way of acting."*

This is the point at which many a client will try the counselor's patience by "forgetting," or "losing the paper," or "getting too busy." These can all be forms of resistance, and they should not slip by without attention. The person needs to be reminded that, while the counselor can provide help and support, "only you, by your own actions, can resolve this problem situation." If fear is a major factor in the resistance, it may be well to use relaxation techniques (chapter 2) or behavioral rehearsal (chapter 5), perhaps in a small group situation, or indeed any other methods that can help to reduce the person's anxiety.

Review and Refinement

An ongoing part of the problem-solving process, done more consciously once concrete action initiatives are under way, is review and refinement. It is important constantly to evaluate the new behavior's effectiveness in achieving the stated goals. Where the review discloses progress, the client will be encouraged to proceed. Where the review discloses lack of progress, the goals themselves may need fresh scrutiny, even changing.

Set goals, identify resources, establish alternatives, take action, review the results—this five-step method is itself subject to refinement. Indeed, the best way to teach problem-solving methods is to help clients actually resolve the problems they bring to you, and then review what you and they have done. Although problem solving can be taught in the office or classroom, people learn it best from concrete experience, while being guided through problems of their own.

Thought Stopping

Jessica Walters, a fifty-three-year-old grandmother, was taking care of her four-year-old grandson one balmy afternoon in the early fall. Hearing the screech of brakes in front of her house, she rushed outside to see Ricky sprawled on the pavement next to the twisted remains of his tricycle.

After five days in the hospital and two weeks convalescing at home, Ricky was as good as new. Jessica was not so lucky. She had trouble sleeping and eating, and from morning to night she chastised herself for being the cause of Ricky's misfortune. On previous occasions when he had visited her house and wanted to go outside, she had said, "Ricky, you be careful and don't play in the street." But on that fateful day she was busy and had gone upstairs for a moment. By the time she returned he was already outside playing. Not more than five minutes later the car struck.

Jessica's self-recrimination had been going on for two months. Her son and daughter-in-law had forgiven her, Ricky had no side effects except a little more respect for motor vehicles, and she had prayed fervently every day since the accident. Yet she continued to go over the event again and again in her mind. Finally the child's mother suggested that Jessica see her pastor.

Jerry Charles knew the events well, having visited the child and his parents in the hospital several times. At first Pastor Charles tried to play down Jessica's problem, but he soon realized that the traditional approach of prayer, forgiveness, and absolution were not enough. Together he and Jessica explored her feelings; this brought understanding and insight, and Jessica agreed that there was no reason for her to continue feeling guilty. Nonetheless her obsessive memories of the accident continued. Pastor Charles at this point made a decision to use the behavioral method called thought stopping.

Thought stopping is a mode of treatment for anxious individuals who have obsessive, ruminative thoughts they seem unable to dispel. After explaining the procedure to Jessica, the pastor had her sit back in a chair and relax with her eyes closed. He then asked her to think of and visualize eating from a bowl of fruit, a common image which posed no threat. As soon as she had the thought fully developed, she was to indicate it by raising her left index finger. At that moment he yelled loudly "Stop!" Thus began her practice of thought stopping. After repeating the procedure four or five times and then taking a few practice runs with other innocuous images, and after Jessica was beginning to feel comfortable with the method, he had her think her obsessive thought about Ricky. She indicated the thought by raising her left index finger, and again Pastor Charles yelled loudly "Stop!"

It is impossible to think two divergent things at the same time. For one moment the obsessive thought is banished—displaced by the loud yell "Stop." After each presentation Pastor Charles asked Jessica if the thought had disappeared, at least for a short time. When she reported that it had, he responded, "Good. Each time this is practiced you will become better and better at being able to dispel your unwanted thoughts."

After a number of presentations in which Pastor Charles yelled "Stop," he asked Jessica to shout it herself when she thought about the accident. After she was proficient at that and reported dispelling the unwanted thought, he instructed her to yell "Stop" in her mind only, without saying anything out loud. In repeated exercises she alternated between saying "Stop" verbally and saying it only in her mind. Eventually she became comfortable and assured in doing it either way. Finally, when she was able momentarily to dispel the obsessive thought at will, she was instructed to do it only subvocally. In this too she succeeded.

Pastor Charles sent Jessica away that day with two homework assignments: She was to practice thought stopping for five minutes three times a day, purposely bringing up thoughts about Ricky's accident and then banishing them with the thought-stopping procedure. She was also to use thought stopping every time the obsessive thought came upon her involuntarily.

When Jessica came in for a second session, one of Pastor Charles's initial questions was, "How did the thought stopping go?" "Only fair," she reported, admitting that she wasn't sure it would help and that she didn't practice much. This is a common response of clients. Thought stopping seems magical, and they don't believe in magic. Pastor Charles, instead of scolding Jessica or abandoning the method, repeated most of what he had done in the previous session, further reinforcing it. He then urged her to practice it again and told her about other people who had used it successfully. They practiced the thought stopping once more during the session, and the pastor asked Jessica for any questions she might have.

On her return for a third session, Jessica reported great success. Her ruminative thoughts had decreased considerably. She was able to banish the agonizing memories for longer and longer periods of time.

Pastor Charles saw Jessica several times more to check on her progress with the thought stopping and to introduce ancillary counseling methods until she was free of her obsession. Thought stopping is usually more beneficial when used in conjunction with other therapeutic and anxiety-reduction techniques. In such a context it becomes an effective and easily taught counseling method.

Thought stopping, of course, is *not* thought repression and is not effective if used as such. To repress the thought is to drive it underground where it can fester and do greater emotional damage. To stop the thought is to face it and deal with it and gradually master it.

Carla Moen, a young television producer, was working on a series of short documentaries for public television. Her colleague on the project was an older and more experienced woman. As the work advanced and duties multiplied and deadlines approached, Carla, a physically healthy person, began to have symptoms of severe stress, including shortness of breath, stomach trouble, dizziness, insomnia, forgetfulness, reduction of her ability to think clearly, and obsessive thoughts about the money they had spent and the mountain of work ahead.

When her colleague left town for ten days on business, the break in routine gave Carla time to assess the situation. She shared her trapped and anxious feelings with her pastor. Carla saw that she had been allowing her partner to dominate the relationship and push her into a project that was more ambitious and demanding than she wanted so early in her career. Her work was conflicting with other things that she valued in life: her family, her friends, her music—she was an accomplished amateur violinist. Learning to be assertive in relation to the men she worked with, she had failed to assert her own wishes and goals over against this woman colleague whom she so much admired and respected.

With the help of Pastor Miller's more dispassioned insights, Carla put her finger on the problem. She then decided that she must have a talk with her colleague, raise these issues, and make some changes in their partnership. She carefully listed the problems and possible solutions, and even wrote an agenda for the meeting with her coproducer.

But it would be six days before Carla would see her partner, and she was experiencing acute distress. She repeatedly agonized over "what a doormat I have been." She rehearsed over and over in her mind what she would say to the woman when the confrontation did finally occur. She was sleeping little, if at all, and her physical symptoms were as bad or worse than before.

In a book Pastor Miller had given her, Carla read a chapter about the thought-stopping techniques described above. Lying awake and agitated at two A.M., she skipped over the first few steps and began silently yelling "Stop!" to herself every time her project or her colleague or their upcoming confrontation came into her consciousness. In no time she was asleep, helped by the thought-stopping method—but also by her belief that it would work! Since the procedure made sense to her, she betrayed none of Jessica's resistance to it.

Five days later Carla met with her collaborator and cleared

the air. She was rested beforehand and relatively calm and, having banished her obsessive thoughts about the meeting, needed only a quick review of the agenda to be on top of the situation. Her colleague, as it turned out, had no desire to be so dominant in the relationship. She willingly agreed to the new ground rules Carla requested. Since they were both conflict avoiders by habit, they agreed in the future to bring up their disagreements immediately. The relationship—and the TV series—was saved, though changed. Two weeks later Carla went back for some renegotiation and this time was able to limit her future involvement in the project to a tolerable two months more.

If Carla had used thought repression, the relationship with her colleague, Carla feels, would have deteriorated to the point where it was past saving—and Carla's own emotional state would probably have been so shaky that she would have had to be hospitalized. On the other hand, after she had faced her feelings and projected a solution to the problem, the thought-stopping technique enabled her to banish those thoughts that were useless to her. She was able to get some sleep, gain some emotional distance, and be at her best while negotiating the necessary changes in a professional relationship that she valued.

Carla's pastor, fortunately, recognized that she had both the intelligence and the motivation to solve her own problems, that all she needed from him was an objective viewpoint and some useful information. It is a mistake in any type of counseling, but especially in behavior therapy, for the pastor to believe that the client is necessarily a weak and helpless creature, dependent on the pastor and subject to the pastor's control.

There are a variety of other behavioral methods in use today that could not be covered in this book. Several which the pastoral counselor might profitably consider are: sexual dysfunction therapy, assertiveness training, covert sensation, and training in interpersonal communication.

The Treatment of Raymond Carlson: A Conclusion

In chapter 1, you will remember, Pastor Harold Jacob visited informally with Raymond Carlson, a parishioner who had come to discuss his son's excessive drinking prior to a youth meeting at the church. At that first session, Raymond had poured out his heart, telling of the pressures in his life and work and the lack of support he felt from his family and from his traditional beliefs in God.

During that visit Raymond had been instructed to do some assessment of what triggers or cues were setting off his disturbed feelings. At the same time, he committed himself to taking action and not just talking about his feelings. He also contracted for three more formal counseling sessions with his pastor. In those subsequent sessions the minister not only offered an empathetic ear; he used with Raymond the specific behavioral methods of relaxation, cognitive restructuring, and problem solving.

In the matter of assessment Raymond and his pastor determined that he was at once under extensive pressure at home and work, and in both places bored and without challenge. In connection with relaxation training Pastor Jacob asked if there were any things in Raymond's life that he had consistently found calming. Raymond mentioned a regular exercise regimen of calisthenics and running, as well as his hobby of working with model airplanes. He was urged to take up both activities again right now, even though he felt he did not have the time to do so, because "often a person who is relaxed can think more clearly and accomplish more tasks than an individual who is anxious and feeling pressured." So Raymond did what was suggested and quickly began to experience a measure of relief.

It was next suggested that Raymond begin catching and identifying his irrational thoughts, and practice cognitive restructuring. Raymond was especially challenged by the section in *A New Guide to Rational Living* which dealt with self-discipline, as well as the idea that happiness is not something that comes to each of us but something we must seek out.* This paralleled what had originally been discussed in the sermon some weeks before, the one which had started Raymond thinking about the meaning of his life.

Problem solving was the next step. If Raymond was, as their assessment indicated, both bored and under extensive pressure (largely self-caused, as he realized from reading Ellis), then he had to make some changes in his life—changes in how he approached his job, and changes in his discretionary time. Raymond and Pastor Jacob both saw that this required, at home, that he and his wife sit down and talk about their relationship, his boredom in it, and his feeling of impotence in the raising of the children. As a result of their talking together, the two of them also began sharing new experiences together, and his wife relinquished some of the fun activities of child rearing to Raymond while he shared with her some of the disciplinary authority.

On the job, Raymond quickly arranged what he called a summit conference with his boss to describe the bind in which he found himself—caught between boss and staff—and also the lack of positive challenge he sensed in his work. This led ultimately, some four months later, to a new position in the company for Raymond, but in the short term it resulted in some specific changes in how his job was structured and how he chose to deal with his staff. For one thing, he determined to take less responsibility for their mistakes and to make each of them more personally accountable.

As a result of these actions in two sectors of his life, Raymond immediately began to feel less pressure and to experience greater joy on all fronts. He felt more comfortable at church and in his relationship with God, but he also realized that he had to take responsibility for his own quest for meaning in life. This became one of the new challenges in his life. Pastor Jacob suggested some readings for his religious growth and also urged him to take one or two courses in theology at a local lay academy. Life for Raymond did not suddenly become a bowl of cherries, but it did become more satisfying and manageable.

As it turned out, that first meeting, set up to discuss his son's drinking, marked the beginning of a very important transition in Raymond's life, a change which had an impact far beyond the four not-too-intensive counseling sessions he completed with his pastor. For him it was a turning point. In just a few sessions he had learned enough to turn a corner, begin reestablishing meaning in his life, and find renewal of joy, peace, and faith.

Raymond's treatment was not magical. His case was not bizarre. There are in fact many people, perhaps in your own home and congregation, who are experiencing the same frustrations and loss of hope. They can also experience a similar reorientation. Readers may even wish to apply the methods here described to their own personal difficulties. Used with a minister's special sensitivity to people's religious struggles, these behavioral methods could help many, like Raymond, to turn a corner and get going on their own quest for meaning and fulfillment in life.

Notes

Page

4. *See the earlier volume in this series by John B. Cobb, Jr., *Theology and Pastoral Care* (Philadelphia: Fortress Press, 1977).
6. *Marvin R. Goldfried and Gerald C. Davison, *Clinical Behavioral Therapy* (New York: Holt, Rinehart & Winston, 1976).
7. *LeRoy Aden, "Pastoral Counseling as Christian Perspective," in *The Dialogue between Theology and Psychology,* ed. Peter Homans (Chicago: University of Chicago Press, 1968), 3:174.
10. *Albert Bandura, *Principles of Behavior Modification* (New York: Holt, Rinehart & Winston, 1969).
12. *For further explanation of rational-emotive therapy, see chapter 3 below, as well as Albert A. Ellis and Robert A. Harper, *A New Guide to Rational Living* (Los Angeles: Wilshire Book Co., 1975).
12. †The reader will note other variations between behavior therapy and other methods as the book progresses. The purpose of this book is not to compare and contrast behavior therapy with other approaches to therapy. An excellent job of this was done by Paul Wachtel, *Action and Insight* (New York: Basic Books, 1976).
17. *See Edmund Jacobson, *Progressive Relaxation* (Chicago: University of Chicago Press, 1929).
17. †See Joseph Wolpe, "The Systematic Desensitization Treatment of Neuroses," in *Experiments in Behaviour Therapy,* ed. H. J. Eysenck (Oxford: Pergamon Press, 1964). For further information about systematic desensitization, see chapter 5 below.
18. *This method is based on Jacobson, *Relaxation,* as well as on Goldfried and Davison, *Therapy*; Spender Rathus and Jeffrey Nevid, *BT: Behavioral Therapy Strategies for Solving Problems in Living* (New York: Doubleday & Co., 1977); Gary Grassi, a Phoenix biofeedback training specialist; and my own clinical experience.
21. *This transcript is based on Johannes H. Schultz and Wolfgang Luthe, *Autogenic Training* (New York: Grune & Stratton, 1959), as well as on Gary Grassi, and my own clinical experience.
23. *Based on Goldfried and Davison, *Therapy,* p. 88.
29. *Rathus and Nevid, *Strategies,* p. 7.
32. *Ellis and Harper, *Rational Living,* pp. 18–29.
33. *See Alberti, *Your Perfect Right,* in the Annotated Bibliography. See also the earlier volume in this series by David W. Augsburger, *Anger and Assertiveness in Pastoral Care* (Philadelphia: Fortress Press, 1979).
34. *Albert Ellis describes the irrational ideas in a variety of ways and a variety of sources One of the best discussions is found in Ellis and Harper, *Rational Living,* pp. 88–195.
35. *For empirical support of this view, see Goldfried and Davison, *Therapy,* p. 161.

35. †Ellis and Harper, *Rational Living,* pp. 18–29.
37. *For example, Ellis and Harper, *Rational Living;* Paul A. Hauck, *Reason in Pastoral Counseling* (Philadelphia: Westminster Press, 1972) and *Overcoming Depression* (Philadelphia: Westminster Press, 1973); or a sheet listing the irrational beliefs.
37. †Ellis and Harper, *Rational Living,* pp. 18–29.
38. *For examples of the effective use of confrontation, see Bernard G. Berenson and Kevin M. Mitchell, *Confrontation for Better or Worse* (Amherst: Human Resource Development Press, 1974).
43. *Ellis and Harper, *Rational Living.*
43. †Paul A. Hauck, *Overcoming Depression; Overcoming Worry and Fear* (Philadelphia: Westminster Press, 1975); *Overcoming Frustration and Anger* (Philadelphia: Westminster Press, 1974).
45. *Gerald R. Patterson, *Families* (Champaign, Ill.: Research Press Co., 1974).
45. †Behavior therapy for children developed from the work of learning theorists, particularly B. F. Skinner. Skinner, one of the most famous psychologists of this century, during the 1930s and 1940s did considerable research on animals. The 1950s were characterized by a shift to a study of humans and the development of therapy techniques. See B. F. Skinner, *Science and Human Behavior* (New York: Macmillan Publishing Co., 1953).
46. *Thomas Gordon, *Parent Effectiveness Training* (New York: Peter H. Wyden, 1970), pp. 29–138.
46. †In conjoint marriage and family counseling the counselor interviews the total family as a unit rather than seeing individuals separately. The assumption is that changes in one person will affect the total family system. One of the best books on the subject is *Conjoint Family Therapy* by Virginia Satir (Palo Alto, Calif.: Science and Behavior Books, 1967).
48. *For further information see in the Annotated Bibliography the two books by Patterson and the books by Rettig and Krumboltz.
65. *Marvin R. Goldfried, "Systematic Desensitization as Training in Self-Control," *Journal of Consulting and Clinical Psychology* 37 (1971): 228–34.
65. †Ibid., p. 232.
67. *Gregory Ziboorg and George W. Henry, *A History of Medical Psychology* (New York: W. W. Norton & Co., 1941).
71. *See the earlier volume in this series by Howard W. Stone, *Crisis Counseling* (Philadelphia: Fortress Press, 1976), pp. 42 ff.
73. *O. Hobart Mowrer, quoted in Howard J. Clinebell, Jr., *Basic Types of Pastoral Counseling* (Nashville: Abingdon Press, 1966), p. 171.
79. *Ellis and Harper, *Rational Living,* pp. 158–67.

Annotated Bibliography

Alberti, Robert E. and Emmons, Michael L. *Your Perfect Right.* San Luis Obispo, Calif.: Impact Press, 1974. This short, readable book describes methods for learning assertiveness.

Beck, Aaron T. *Cognitive Therapy and the Emotional Disorders.* New York: International Universities Press, 1976. A cognitive approach to counseling that represents a scientific and common-sense understanding of people's emotional disorders.

Ellis, Albert A. and Harper, Robert A. *A New Guide to Rational Living.* Los Angeles: Wilshire Book Co., 1975. The basic and first book to read for gaining an understanding of rational-emotive therapy.

Eysenck, H. J., ed. *Experiments in Behaviour Therapy.* Oxford: Pergamon Press, 1964. Slightly outdated, this volume includes many good chapters which focus especially on systematic desensitization and reinforcement principles.

Goldfried, Marvin R. and Davison, Gerald C. *Clinical Behavior Therapy.* New York: Holt, Rinehart & Winston, 1976. Introduces the reader to behavior therapy, with special attention to relaxation training, systematic desensitization, behavior rehearsal, cognitive restructuring, problem solving, and reinforcement principles.

Grassi, Gary. *Biofeedback Relaxation Training: A 28-Day Cassette Home Training Program.* Scottsdale, Ariz.: Health Awareness Training Programs, 1978. The best materials I have encountered on teaching relaxation, to be used with a cassette tape recorder.

Hauck, Paul A. *Overcoming Depression.* Philadelphia: Westminster Press, 1973. A clear, easily read book applying Ellis' rational-emotive therapy concepts to the treatment of depression.

————. *Reason in Pastoral Counseling.* Philadelphia: Westminster Press, 1972. An attempt to apply Ellis's cognitive therapy to pastoral care.

Knox, David. *Marriage Happiness.* Champaign, Ill.: Research Press Co., 1974. Incorporates behavior therapy methods into the practice of marriage counseling.

Krumboltz, John D. and Krumboltz, Helen B. *Changing Children's Behavior.* Englewood Cliffs, N.J.: Prentice-Hall, 1972. An excellent work on child rearing, using many examples to underline the techniques described.

Lanyon, Richard I. and Lanyon, Barbara P. *Behavior Therapy: A Clinical Introduction.* Reading, Mass.: Addison-Wesley Publishing Co., 1978. An excellent introduction to the practice of behavior therapy.

Leitenberg, Harold, ed. *Handbook of Behavior Modification and Behavior Therapy.* Englewood Cliffs, N.J.: Prentice-Hall, 1976. A problem-oriented behavior therapy book that describes treatment for such problems as depression, overeating, marital difficulties, alcoholism, and sexual disorders.

Patterson, Gerald R. and Gullion, M. Elizabeth. *Living With Children.* Champaign, Ill. Research Press Co., 1971; and Patterson, Gerald R. *Families.* Champaign, Ill.: Research Press Co., 1974. These two books, simply written, give parents practical ways of using behavior therapy methods in handling their children.

Rettig, Edward B. *ABCs for Parents.* Van Nuys, Calif.: Associates for Behavior Change, 1973. Details methods for using behavior therapy with children.

Schultz, Johannes H. and Luthe, Wolfgang. *Autogenic Therapy.* Vols. 1–3. New York: Grune & Stratton, 1969. The originators of autogenic training explain this method of training people in relaxation.

Stone, Howard W. *Crisis Counseling.* Philadelphia: Fortress Press, 1976. Chapter 2 describes crises in cognitive behavioral terms, and chapter 3 has a fairly detailed description of problem-solving methods.